THE

NATIONAL SUNDAY LAW,

ARGUMENT OF

ALONZO T. JONES

BEFORE THE

United States Senate Committee on Education and Labor;

AT

WASHINGTON, D. C., DEC. 13, 1888.

TEACH Services, Inc.
Brushton, New York

Copyright © 2002 TEACH Services, Inc.

ISBN 1-57258-056-9
Library of Congress Catalog Card No. 95-61511

Facsimile Reproduction

This historical classic has been reproduced in its original form. Frequent
variations in the quality of the print are unavoidable due to the condition
of the original. Thus the print may look lighter and appear to be missing
detail, more in some places than in others.

Published by

TEACH Services, Inc.
www.tsibooks.com

INTRODUCTION.

THIS pamphlet is a report of an argument made upon the national Sunday bill introduced by Senator Blair in the fiftieth Congress. It is not, however, exactly the argument that was made before the Senate Committee, as there were so many interruptions in the course of my speech that it was impossible to make a connected argument upon a single point. By these questions, etc., my argument was not only forced to take a wider range than was intended when I began to speak, but I was prevented from making the definite argument that I designed to present. I do not speak of these interruptions and counter-arguments by way of complaint, but only to explain why this pamphlet is issued. Nevertheless it is a fact that while there were eighteen speeches before mine, occupying three hours, in all of which together there were only one hundred and eighty-nine questions and counter-arguments by all the members of the Committee who were present, I was interrupted by the Chairman alone, *one hundred and sixty-nine times* in *ninety* minutes, as may be seen by the official report of the hearing.—*Fiftieth Congress, Second Session, Messages and Documents No. 43, pp. 73–102.*

A national Sunday law is a question of national interest. While it is true that the Sunday-rest bill did not become a law, the legislation having died with the expiration of the fiftieth Congress, it is also true that those who worked for the introduction and passage of that bill are now laying plans to have another national

(iii)

what prevented them?

Sunday bill introduced as soon as possible in the fifty-
first Congress, and will do all in their power to secure
its enactment into law. The scope that was given to
the subject by the questions asked of me by the Senate
Committee, has opened the way for a somewhat ex-
haustive treatment of the subject. These questions
being raised by United States senators, — men of national affairs, — show that a wider circulation of this
matter is not out of place. The subject is worthy of
the careful attention of the whole American people.
The principles of the American Constitution, the proper
relationship between religion and the State, the distinction between moral and civil law, the inalienable civil
and religious rights of men, — these are questions that
never should become secondary in the mind of any
American citizen.

An eminent American jurist has justly observed
that in a government of the people "there is no
safety except in an enlightened public opinion, based
on individual intelligence." Constitutional provisions
against the encroachments of the religious upon the
civil power are safeguards only so long as the intelligence of the people shall recognize the truth that no
man can allow any legislation in behalf of the religion, or the religious observances, in which he himself
believes, without forfeiting his own religious freedom.

In enlarging as I have upon the matter presented in
the original hearing, the meaning or intention of any
statement has not been changed in the slightest degree.
The argument is submitted to the American people
with the earnest hope that they will give thoughtful
consideration to the principles involved. The positions
taken will bear the severest test of every form of just
criticism.

marriage about — our liberties are in jeopardy — ever since 9-11-01 They've telegraphed it.

is many a civil institution to be protected

how can a man be so sure — hisself — he was out of line + wentwrong had to — using logic — ? sounds like Etifner a man who is perfect in EG — he + we gone know is to overstate tigs. b/f you — I have the breath of god.

The bill proposed by Senator Blair, and upon which the argument was made, is as follows : —

> "50th CONGRESS, } S. 2983.
> 1st SESSION. }

"IN the Senate of the United States, May 21, 1888, Mr. Blair introduced the following bill, which was read twice, and referred to the Committee on Education and Labor : —

"A bill to secure to the people the enjoyment of the first day of the week, commonly known as the Lord's day, as a day of rest, and to promote its observance as a day of religious worship. *Cath. Cardinal's supported it.*

"*Be it enacted by the Senate and House of Representatives of the United States of America in Congress assembled,* That no person, or corporation, or the agent, servant, or employee of any person or corporation, shall perform or authorize to be performed any secular work, labor, or business to the disturbance of others, works of necessity, mercy, and humanity excepted; nor shall any person engage in any play, game, or amusement, or recreation, to the disturbance of others, on the first day of the week, commonly known as the Lord's day, or during any part thereof, in any territory, district, vessel, or place subject to the exclusive jurisdiction of the United States; nor shall it be lawful for any person or corporation to receive pay for labor or service performed or rendered in violation of this section.

"SEC. 2. That no mails or mail matter shall hereafter be transported in time of peace over any land postal route, nor shall any mail matter be collected, assorted, handled, or delivered during any part of the first day of the week: *Provided,* That whenever any letter shall relate to a work of necessity or mercy, or shall concern the health, life, or decease of any person, and the fact shall be plainly stated upon the face of the envelope containing the same, the postmaster-general shall provide for the transportation of such letter.

"SEC. 3. That the prosecution of commerce between the States and with the Indian tribes, the same not being work of necessity, mercy, or humanity, by the transportation of persons or property by land or water in such way as to interfere with or disturb the people in the enjoyment of the first day of the week, or any portion thereof, as a day of rest from labor, the same not being labor of necessity, mercy, or humanity, or its observance as a day of religious worship, is hereby prohibited; and any person or corporation, or the agent or employee of any person or corporation, who shall willfully violate this section, shall be punished by a fine of not less than ten nor more than one thousand dollars, and no service performed in the prosecution of such prohibited commerce shall be lawful, nor shall any compensation be recoverable or be paid for the same.

"SEC. 4. That all military and naval drills, musters, and parades, not in time of active service or immediate preparation therefor, of soldiers, sailors, marines, or cadets of the United States, on the first day of the week, except assemblies for the due and orderly observance of religious worship, are hereby prohibited, nor shall any unnecessary labor be performed or permitted in the military or naval service of the United States on the Lord's day.

"SEC. 5. That it shall be unlawful to pay or to receive payment or wages in any manner for service rendered, or for labor performed, or for the transportation of persons or of property in violation of the provisions of this act, nor shall any action lie for the recovery thereof, and when so paid, whether in advance or otherwise, the same may be recovered back by whoever shall first sue for the same.

"SEC. 6. That labor or service performed and rendered on the first day of the week in consequence of accident, disaster, or unavoidable delays in making the regular connections upon postal routes and routes of travel and transportation, the preservation of perishable and exposed property, and the regular and necessary transportation and delivery of articles of food in condition for healthy use, and such transportation for short distances from one State, district, or Territory, into another State, district, or Territory as by local laws shall be declared to be necessary for the public good, shall not be deemed violations of this act, but the same shall be construed, so far as possible, to secure to the whole people rest from toil during the first day of the week, their mental and moral culture, and the religious observance of the Sabbath day."

Rev. A. H. Lewis, D. D., representative of the Seventh-day Baptists, had spoken, and asked that a section be added to the bill granting exemption to observers of the Seventh day; but in answering the questions that were asked by the Chairman, Mr. Lewis compromised his position, and was followed soon after by Dr. Herrick Johnson, of Chicago, who remarked that Dr. Lewis had "given his whole case away." This is what is referred to in my introductory remarks to the effect that we did not intend to "give *our* case away."   A. T. J.

what of the civil laws relating to marriage wh/is both
a civil contract + a relig. institution?
→ why marry if hardly any are happy? — (ie agrees + fight)
God seeks godly offspring - the children are the future
of the state.

CONTENTS.

Constantine's
321 AD →
1st Sunday
law

[viii]

[handwritten marginalia at top of page:]

Problems in marr/
1) spending money – indebtedness
= slavery — we still have legalized
slavery / indentured servitude
2) sexual problems
3) lack of love
– performance is/ called marriage!
– willingness to fulfill other partner's needs
– boredom – lack of excitement
– socially incompatible
– demanding partner
– physically incompatible
– growing apart – intellectually, physically
socially etc where 1 partner does not contribute
to grow –

THE NATIONAL SUNDAY LAW.

ARGUMENT OF ALONZO T. JONES BEFORE THE SENATE
COMMITTEE, WASHINGTON, D. C.

Senator Blair. — There are gentlemen present who wish to be heard in opposition to the bill. Prof. Alonzo T. Jones, of Battle Creek College, Mich., is one of those who have spoken to me in regard to it. Will you not state, Prof. Jones, what your desire is? I have no doubt that we can obtain leave of the Senate to sit during its session to-day. It is exceedingly desirable to go on with this hearing, and complete it now. How would such an arrangement comport with your convenience? First, state, please, whom you represent, and your reasons for desiring to be heard.

Mr. Jones. — Mr. Chairman, I represent the people known as Seventh-day Adventists. It is true, we have been entirely ignored by the other side. The very small "*sect*," as they stated it, of Seventh-day Baptists has been recognized, but we are more than three times their number, and many times their power in the real force of our work. We have organizations in every State and Territory in the Union. We have the largest printing-house in Michigan; the largest printing-house on the Pacific Coast; the largest Sanitarium in the world; a college in California and one in Michigan; an academy in Massachusetts; a printing establishment in Basel, Switzerland; one in Christiana,

[handwritten marginalia at right:] extent / your / work – / ignored by / several / legislature / please

Norway; and one in Melbourne, Australia. Our mission work has enlarged until, besides embracing the greater part of Europe, it has also extended nearly around the world; and we desire a hearing, with the consent of the Committee.

Senator Blair. — Where do you reside?

Mr. Jones. — At present in Michigan. My home for the past four years has been in California. I am now teaching history in Battle Creek College, Mich.

I must say in justice to myself, and also in behalf of the body which I represent, that we dissent almost wholly, I might say, wholly, from the position taken by the representative of the Seventh-day Baptists. I knew, the instant that Dr. Lewis stated what he did here, that he had "given his case away." We have not given our case away, Senators, nor do we expect to give it away. We expect to go deeper than any have gone at this hearing, both upon the principles and upon the facts, as well as upon the logic of the facts.

Senator Blair. — This matter is all familiar to you. You are a professor of history. Can you not go on this afternoon?

Mr. Jones. — Yes, if I can have a little space between now and this afternoon to get my papers together. I have some references to read that I did not bring with me this morning.

Senator Blair. — Very well.

ARGUMENT.

Senator Blair. — You have a full hour, Professor. It is now half past one.

Mr. Jones. — There are three particular lines in which I wish to conduct the argument: First, the principles upon which we stand; second, the historical view; and, third, the practical aspect of the question.

The principle upon which we stand is that civil government is civil, and has nothing to do in the matter of legislation, with religious observances in any way. The basis of this is found in the words of Jesus Christ in Matt. 22 : 21. When the Pharisees asked whether it was lawful to give tribute to Cæsar or not, he replied: "Render therefore unto Cæsar the things which are Cæsar's; and unto God the things that are God's."

In this the Saviour certainly separated that which pertains to Cæsar from that which pertains to God. We are not to render to Cæsar that which pertains to God; we are not to render to God by Cæsar that which is God's.

Senator Blair. — May not the thing due to Cæsar be due to God also?

Mr. Jones. — No, sir. If that be so, then the Saviour did entangle himself in his talk, the very thing which they wanted him to do. The record says that they sought "how they might entangle him in his talk." Having drawn the distinction which he has, between that which belongs to Cæsar and that which belongs to God, if it be true that the same things belong to both, then he did entangle himself in his talk; and where is the force in his words which command us to render to Cæsar that which belongs to Cæsar, and to God the things that are God's?

Senator Blair. — Is it not a requirement of God's that we render to Cæsar that which is due to Cæsar?

Mr. Jones. — Yes.

Senator Blair. — If Cæsar is *society*, and the Sabbath is required for the good of society, does not God require us to establish the Sabbath for the good of society? and if society makes a law accordingly, is it not binding?

Mr. Jones. — It is for the good of society that men shall be Christians ; but it is not in the province of the State to make Christians. For the State to undertake to do so would not be for the benefit of society ; it never has been, and it never can be.

Senator Blair. — Do you not confuse this matter? A thing may be required for the good of society, and for that very reason be in accordance with the will and the command of God. God issues his commands for the good of society, does he not? God does not give us commands that have no relation to the good of society.

Mr. Jones. — His commands are for the good of man.

Senator Blair. — Man is society. It is made up of individual men.

Mr. Jones. — But in that which God has issued to man for the good of men he has given those things which pertain solely to man's relationship to his God ; and he has also given things which pertain to man's relationship to his fellow-men. With those things in which our duty pertains to our fellow-men, civil government can have something to do.

Senator Blair. — Man would obey God in obeying civil society.

Mr. Jones. — I will come to that point. In the things which pertain to our duty to God, with the individual's right of serving God as one's conscience dictates, society has nothing to do ; but in the formation of civil society, there are certain rights surrendered to the society by the individual, without which society could not be organized.

Senator Blair. — That is not conceded. When was this doctrine of a compact in society made? It is the philosophy of an infidel.

Mr. Jones. It is made wherever you find men together.

Senator Blair. — Did you and I ever agree to it? Did it bind us before we were *compos mentis?*

Mr. Jones. — Certainly. Civil government is an ordinance of God.

Senator Blair. — Then it is not necessarily an agreement of man?

Mr. Jones. — Yes, sir, it springs from the people.

Senator Blair. — As to the compact in society that is talked about, it is not conceded that it is a matter of personal and individual agreement. Society exists altogether independent of the volition of those who enter into it. However, I shall not interrupt you further. I only did this because of our private conversation, in which I thought you labored under a fallacy in your fundamental proposition, that would lead all the way through your argument. I suggested that ground, and that is all.

Mr. Jones. — I think the statement of the Declaration of Independence is true, that "Governments derive their just powers from the consent of the governed."

Senator Blair. — I do not controvert that.

Mr. Jones. — Of all men in the world, Americans ought to be the last to deny the social compact theory of civil government. On board the "Mayflower," before the Pilgrim Fathers ever set foot on these shores, the following was written : —

"In the name of God, Amen. We, whose names are underwritten, the loyal subjects of our dread sovereign,

Lord King James, by the grace of God, of Great Britain, France, and Ireland, king, defender of the faith, etc., having undertaken for the glory of God, and advancement of the Christian faith, and the honor of our king and country, a voyage to plant the first colony in the northern parts of Virginia ; *do by these presents, solemnly and mutually,* in the presence of God and one another, *covenant and combine ourselves together into a civil body politick,* for our better ordering and preservation, and furtherance of the ends aforesaid : and by virtue hereof do enact, constitute, and frame such just and equal laws, ordinances, acts, constitutions, and officers, from time to time, as shall be thought most meet and convenient for the general good of the colony ; unto which we promise all due submission and obedience. In witness whereof we have hereunto subscribed our names at Cape Cod, the eleventh of November, in the reign of our sovereign, Lord King James, of England, France, and Ireland, the eighteenth, and of Scotland, the fiftyfourth, Anno Domini, 1620.'

The next American record is that of the fundamental orders of Connecticut, 1638–39, and reads as follows : —

" Forasmuch as it hath pleased the Allmighty God by the wise disposition of his diuyne pruidence so to order and dispose of things that we, the inhabitants and residents of Windsor, and Harteford, and Wethersfield, are now cohabiting and dwelling in and vppon the river of Conectecotte and the lands thereunto adioyneing ; and well knowing where a people are gathered together the word of God requires that to mayntayne the peace and vnion of such a people there should be an orderly and decent gourment established acording to God, to order and dispose of the affayres of the people at all seasons, as occation shall require ; *doe therefore assotiate and conioyne ourselues to be as one publike State or commonwelth ;* and doe *for ourselues and our successors and such as shall adioyned to vs att any tyme hereafter, enter into combination and confederation together,*" etc.

And, sir, the first Constitution of your own State —
1784 — in its bill of rights, declares : —

"I. All men are born equally free and independent ;
therefore, all government of right originates from the
people, *is founded in consent*, and instituted for the general good."

"III. When men enter into a state of society, they
surrender some of their natural rights to that society,
in order to insure the protection of others ; and without such an equivalent, the surrender is void.

"IV. Among the natural rights, some are in their
very nature unalienable, because no equivalent can be
received for them. Of this kind are the rights of conscience."

And in Part 2, of that same Constitution, under
the division of the "form of government," are these
words : —

"The people inhabiting the territory formerly called
the province of New Hampshire, do *hereby solemnly and
mutually agree with each other* to form themselves into
a free, sovereign, and independent body politic, or
State, by the name of the State of New Hampshire."

In the Constitution of New Hampshire of 1792, these
articles are repeated word for word. They remain
there without alteration in a single letter under the ratification of 1852, and also under the ratification of 1877.
Consequently, sir, the very State which sends you to
this capitol is founded upon the very theory which
you here deny. This is the doctrine of the Declaration
of Independence ; it is the doctrine of the Scripture ;
and therefore we hold it to be eternally true.

These sound and genuine American principles —
civil governments deriving their just powers from the
consent of the governed, and the inalienability of the

rights of conscience,— these are the principles asserted and maintained by Seventh-day Adventists.

Senator Blair. — But society is behind the government which society creates.

Mr. Jones.—Certainly.   All civil government springs from the people, I care not in what form it is.

Senator Blair. — That is all agreed to.

Mr. Jones.— But the people, I care not how many there are, have no right to invade your relationship to God, nor mine.   That rests between the individual and God, through faith in Jesus Christ ; and as the Saviour has made this distinction between that which pertains to Cæsar and that which is God's, when Cæsar exacts of men that which pertains to God, then Cæsar is out of his place, and in so far as Cæsar is obeyed there, God is denied.   When Cæsar — civil government — exacts of men that which is God's, he demands what does not belong to him ; in so doing Cæsar usurps the place and the prerogative of God, and every man who regards God or his own rights before God, will disregard all such interference on the part of Cæsar.

This argument is confirmed by the apostle's commentary upon Christ's words.   In Rom. 13 : 1–9, is written :—

"Let every soul be subject unto the higher powers. For there is no power but of God : the powers that be are ordained of God.   Whosoever therefore resisteth the power, resisteth the ordinance of God : and they that resist shall receive to themselves damnation.   For rulers are not a terror to good works, but to the evil.   Wilt thou then not be afraid of the power ? do that which is good, and thou shalt have praise of the same : for he is the minister of God to thee for good.   But if thou do that which is evil, be afraid ; for he beareth not the sword in vain : for he is the minister of God, a revenger to execute wrath upon him that doeth evil.   Wherefore ye must needs be subject not only for wrath, but also for conscience' sake. For, for this cause pay ye tribute also : for they are God's ministers, attending continually upon this very thing. Render therefore to all their dues : tribute to whom tribute is due ; custom to whom custom ; fear to whom fear ; honor to whom honor. Owe no man any thing, but to love one another : for he that loveth another hath fulfilled the law. For this, Thou shalt not commit adultery, Thou shalt not kill, Thou shalt not steal, Thou shalt not bear false witness, Thou shalt not covet ; and if there be any other commandment, it is briefly comprehended in this saying, namely, Thou shalt love thy neighbor as thyself."

It is easy to see that this scripture is but an exposition of Christ's words, "Render therefore unto Cæsar the things which are Cæsar's." In the Saviour's command to render unto Cæsar the things that are Cæsar's, there is plainly a recognition of the rightfulness of civil government, and that civil government has claims upon us which we are in duty bound to recognize, and that there are things which duty requires us to render to the civil government. This scripture in Romans 13 simply states the same thing in other words : "Let every soul be subject unto the higher powers. For there is no power but of God : the powers that be are ordained of God."

Again : the Saviour's words were in answer to a question concerning tribute. They said to him, "Is it lawful to give tribute unto Cæsar, or not ?" Rom. 13 : 6 refers to the same thing, saying, "For, for this cause pay ye tribute also : for they are God's ministers, attending continually upon this very thing." In answer to the question of the Pharisees about the tribute, Christ said, "Render therefore unto Cæsar the things which are Cæsar's." Rom. 13 : 7, taking up the same thought, says, "Render therefore to all their dues :

tribute to whom tribute is due ; custom to whom custom ; fear to whom fear ; honor to whom honor."
These references make positive that which we have
stated, — that this portion of Scripture (Rom. 13 : 1–9)
is a divine commentary upon the words of Christ in
Matt. 22 : 17–21.

The passage refers first to civil government, the
higher powers, — the powers that be. Next it speaks
of rulers, as bearing the sword and attending upon
matters of tribute. Then it commands to render tribute to whom tribute is due, and says, "Owe no
man any thing ; but to love one another : for he that
loveth another hath fulfilled the law." Then he refers
to the sixth, seventh, eighth, ninth, and tenth commandments, and says, "If there be any other commandment, it is briefly comprehended in this saying,
namely, Thou shalt love thy neighbor as thyself."

There are other commandments of this same law to
which Paul refers. There are the four commandments
of the first table of the law, — the commandments
which say, "Thou shalt have no other gods before
me ;" "Thou shalt not make unto thee any graven image,
or any likeness of any thing ;" "Thou shalt not take the
name of the Lord thy God in vain ;" "Remember the
Sabbath day to keep it holy." Then there is the other
commandment in which are briefly comprehended all
these, "Thou shalt love the Lord thy God with all thy
heart, and with all thy soul, and with all thy mind, and
with all thy strength."

Paul knew full well these commandments. Why,
then, did he say, "If there be any other commandment,
it is briefly comprehended in this saying, namely, Thou
shalt love thy neighbor as thyself"? — Because he was
writing concerning the principles set forth by the Saviour, which relate to our duties to civil government.

Our duties under civil government pertain solely to the government and to our fellow-men, because the powers of civil government pertain solely to men in their relations one to another, and to the government. But the Saviour's words in the same connection entirely separated that which pertains to God from that which pertains to civil government. The things which pertain to God are not to be rendered to civil government — to the powers that be; therefore Paul, although knowing full well that there were other commandments, said, "If there be any other commandment, it is briefly comprehended in this saying, namely, Thou shalt love thy neighbor as thyself;" that is, if there be any other commandment which comes into the relation between man and civil government, it is comprehended in this saying, that he shall love his neighbor as himself; thus showing conclusively that the powers that be, though ordained of God, are so ordained simply in things pertaining to the relation of man with his fellow-men, and in those things alone.

Further: as in this divine record of the duties that men owe to the powers that be, there is no reference whatever to the first table of the law, it therefore follows that the powers that be, although ordained of God, have nothing whatever to do with the relations which men bear toward God.

As the ten commandments contain the whole duty of man, and as in the enumeration here given of the duties that men owe to the powers that be, there is no mention of any of the things contained in the first table of the law, it follows that none of the duties enjoined in the first table of the law of God, do men owe to the powers that be; that is to say, again, that the powers that be, although ordained of God, are not ordained of God in anything pertaining to a single duty enjoined in any one of the first four of the ten commandments. These are duties that men owe to God, and with these the powers that be can of right have nothing to do, because Christ has commanded to render unto God — not to Cæsar, nor by Cæsar — that which is God's. Therefore, as in his comment upon the principle which Christ established, Paul has left out of the account the first four commandments, so we deny, forever, the right of any civil government to legislate in anything that pertains to men's duty to God under the first four commandments. This Sunday bill does propose to legislate in regard to the Lord's day. If it is the Lord's day, we are to render it to the Lord, not to Cæsar. When Cæsar exacts it of us, he is exacting what does not belong to him, and is demanding of us that with which he should have nothing to do.

Senator Blair. — Would it answer your objection in that regard, if, instead of saying "the Lord's day," we should say, "Sunday"?

Mr. Jones. — No, sir. Because the underlying principle, the sole basis, of Sunday, is ecclesiastical, and legislation in regard to it is ecclesiastical legislation. I shall come more fully to the question you ask, presently.

Now do not misunderstand us on this point. We are Seventh-day Adventists; but if this bill were in favor of enforcing the observance of the seventh day as the Lord's day, we would oppose it just as much as we oppose it as it is now, for the reason that civil government has nothing to do with *what* we owe to God, or whether we *owe* anything or not, or whether we *pay* it or not.

Allow me again to refer to the words of Christ to emphasize this point. At that time the question was upon the subject of tribute, whether it was lawful to give tribute to Cæsar or not. In answering the question, Christ established this principle: "Render therefore unto Cæsar the things which are Cæsar's, and unto God the things that are God's." That tribute money was Cæsar's; it bore his image and superscription; it was to be rendered to him. *Now,* it is a question of rendering Sabbath observance, and it is a perfectly legitimate and indeed a necessary question to ask right here: Is it lawful to render Lord's day observance to Cæsar? The reply may be in His own words: Show me the Lord's day; whose image and superscription does it bear?—The Lord's, to be sure. This very bill which is under discussion here to-day declares it to be the Lord's day. Then the words of Christ apply to this. Bearing the image and superscription of the Lord, Render therefore to the Lord the things that are the Lord's, and to Cæsar the things that are Cæsar's. It does not bear the image and superscription of Cæsar; it does not belong to him; it is not to be rendered to him.

Again: take the institution under the word *Sabbath:* Is it lawful to render Sabbath observance to Cæsar or not? Show us the Sabbath; whose image and superscription does it bear? The commandment of God says, it "is the Sabbath of the Lord thy God." It bears his image and superscription, and his only; it belongs wholly to him; Cæsar can have nothing to do with it. It does not belong to Cæsar; its observance cannot be rendered to Cæsar, but only to God; for the commandment is, "Remember the Sabbath day, *to keep it holy.*" If it is not kept holy, it is not kept at all. Therefore, belonging to God, bearing his superscription, and not that of Cæsar, according to Christ's commandment, it is to be rendered only to God ; because we are to render to God that which is God's, and the Sabbath is the Sabbath of the Lord thy God.   Sabbath observance, therefore, or Lord's day observance, whichever you may choose to call it, never can be rendered to Cæsar.   And Cæsar never can demand it without demanding that which belongs to God, or without putting himself in the place of God, and usurping the prerogative of God.

Therefore, we say that if this bill were framed in behalf of the real Sabbath of the Lord, the seventh day, the day which we observe ; if this bill proposed to promote its observance, or to compel men to do no work upon that day, we would oppose it just as strongly as we oppose it now, and I would stand here at this table and argue precisely as I am arguing against this, and upon the same principle, — the principle established by Jesus Christ, — that with that which is God's the civil government never can of right have anything to do.   That duty rests solely between man and God ; and if any man does not render it to God, he is responsible only to God, and not to any man, nor to any assembly or organization of men, for his failure or refusal to render it to God ; and any power that undertakes to punish that man for his failure or refusal to render to God what is God's, puts itself in the place of God.   Any government which attempts it, sets itself against the word of Christ, and is therefore antichristian.   This Sunday bill proposes to have this Government do just that thing, and therefore I say, without any reflection upon the author of the bill, this national Sunday bill which is under discussion here to-day is *antichristian*.   But in saying this I am not singling out this contemplated law as worse than all other Sunday laws in the world. There never was a Sunday law that was not antichristian, and there never can be one that will not be antichristian.

Senator Blair. — You oppose all the Sunday laws of the country, then?

Mr. Jones. — Yes, sir.

Senator Blair. — You are against all Sunday laws?

Mr. Jones. — Yes, sir; we are against every Sunday law that was ever made in this world, from the first enacted by Constantine to this one now proposed; and we would be equally against a Sabbath law if it were proposed, for that would be antichristian, too.

Senator Blair. — State and national, alike?

Mr. Jones. — State and national, sir. I shall give you historical reasons presently, and the facts upon which these things stand, and I hope they will receive consideration.

George Washington, I believe, is yet held in some respectful consideration — he is by the Seventh-day Adventists at least — and he said, "Every man who conducts himself as a good citizen is accountable alone to God for his religious faith, and is to be protected in worshiping God according to the dictates of his own conscience." And so should we be protected, so long as we are law-abiding citizens. There are no saloon keepers among us. We are as a body for prohibition; and as for the principles of Christian temperance, we conscientiously practice them. In short, you will find no people in this country or in the world, more peaceable and law-abiding than we endeavor to be. We teach the people according to the Scripture, to be subject to the powers that be; we teach them that the highest duty of the Christian *citizen* is strictly to obey the law, — to obey it not from fear of punishment, but out of respect for governmental authority, and out of respect for God, and conscience toward him.

Senator Blair. — That is the common Mormon argument. The Mormons say their institution is a matter of religious belief. Everybody concedes their right to believe in Mormonism, but when they come to the point of practicing it, will it not be to the disturbance of others?

Mr. Jones. — I should have come to that, even though you had not asked the question. But as you have introduced it, I will notice it now. My argument throughout is that the civil government can never have anything to do with men's duties under the first four of the ten commandments; and this is the argument embodied in Washington's words. These duties pertain solely to God. Now polygamy is adultery. But adultery is not a duty that men owe to God, in any way, much less does it come under any of the first four commandments. This comes within the inhibitions of the second table of the law of God — the commandments embracing duty to our neighbor. How men should conduct themselves toward their fellow-men, civil government must decide; that is the very purpose of its existence. Consequently, the practice of polygamy lying wholly within this realm, is properly subject to the jurisdiction of civil government. My argument does not in the least degree countenance the principles of Mormonism, nor can it fairly be made to do so. I know that it is offered as a very ready objection; but those who offer it as an objection and as an argument against the principles upon which we stand, thereby make adultery a religious practice. But against all such objection and argument, I maintain that adultery is not in any sense a religious practice. It is not only highly irreligious, but it is essentially *uncivil;* and because **it is uncivil,** the civil power has as much **right to blot it out as it has** to punish murder, or thieving, or perjury, **or any other** uncivil thing. Moreover, we deny that **honest occupa-** tions on any day of the week, or at any time **whatever,** can ever properly be classed with adultery.

There are also people who believe in **community of** property in this world. Suppose they base **their prin-** ciples of having all things in common upon **the apos-** tolic example. Very good. They have the **right to do** that. Every one who sells his property and puts it into a common fund, has a right to do that if he chooses; but suppose these men in carrying out that principle, and in claiming that it is a religious ordinance, were to take without consent your property or mine into their community. Then what?—The State forbids it. **It** does not forbid the exercise of their religion; but it protects your property and mine, and in exercising its prerogative of protection, it forbids theft. And in for- bidding theft, the State never asks any questions as to whether thieving is a religious practice. So also as to polygamy, which is practiced among the Mormons. But let us consider this in another view.

It is every man's right in this country, or anywhere else, to worship an idol if he chooses. That idol em- bodies his conviction of what God is. He can worship only according to his convictions. It matters not what form his idol may have, he has the right to worship it anywhere in all the world, therefore in the United States. But suppose that in the worship of that god he attempts to take the life of one of his fellow-men, and of- fer it as a human sacrifice. The civil government exists for the protection of life, liberty, property, etc., and it must punish that man for his attempt upon the life of his fellow-man.   The civil law protects man's life from such exercise of any one's religion, but in punishing the offender, the State does not consider the question of his religion at all.   It would punish him just the same if he made no pretensions to worship or to religion.   It punishes him for his incivility, for his attempt at murder, not for his irreligion.   I repeat, the question of religion is not considered by the State ; the sole question is, Did he threaten the life of his fellow-man ?   Civil government must protect its citizens.   This is strictly within Cæsar's jurisdiction ; it comes within the line of duties which the Scripture shows to pertain to our neighbor, and with it Cæsar has to do.

Therefore it is true that the State can never of right legislate in regard to any man's religious faith, or in relation to anything in the first four commandments of the decalogue.   But if in the exercise of his religious convictions under the first four commandments, a man invades the rights of his neighbor, as to life, family, property, or character, then the civil government says that it is unlawful.   Why ?   Because it is irreligious or immoral ? — Not at all ; but because it is uncivil, and for that reason only.   It never can be proper for the State to ask any question as to whether any man is religious or not, or whether his actions are religious or not.   The sole question must ever be, Is the action civil or uncivil.

Senator Blair. — Now apply that right to this case — to the institution of the Sabbath among men for the good of men.

Mr. Jones. — Very good, we will consider that. Here are persons who are keeping Sunday.   It is their right to work on every other day of the week.   It is their right to work on *that* day, if they desire ; but they

are keeping that day, recognizing it as the Sabbath.
Now while they are doing that which is their right,
here are other people who are keeping Saturday, and
others who are keeping Friday. The Mohammedans
recognize Friday. But we will confine ourselves to
those who keep Saturday, the seventh day, as the Sabbath. Those who keep Sunday, and who want legislation for that day, ask that other people shall be forbidden to work on Sunday, because they say it disturbs
their rest, it disturbs their worship, etc.; and they
claim that their rights are not properly protected.
Do they really believe that in principle? Let us see.
They will never admit (at any rate, I have never yet
found one of them who would) that their work on Saturday disturbs the rest, or the worship, of the man who
rests on Saturday. If their work on Saturday does not
disturb the Sabbath rest, or the worship, of the man
who keeps Saturday, then upon what principle is it that
our work on Sunday disturbs the rest of those who keep
Sunday? I have never found one on that side yet who
would admit the principle. If their work does not disturb our rest and our worship, our work *cannot* disturb
their rest or their worship. More than this: In a general Sunday convention held in San Francisco, at which
I was present, there was a person who spoke on this
very question. Said he: "There are some people, and a
good many of them in this State, who do not believe in
Sunday laws, and who keep Saturday as the Sabbath;
but," said he, "the majority must rule. The vast majority of the people do keep Sunday; their rights must
be respected, and they have a right to enact it into
law." I arose and said, "Suppose the Seventh-day
people were in the majority, and they should go to the
legislature and ask for a law to compel you to keep

Saturday out of respect to their rights. Would you consider it right?" There was a murmur all over the house, " No."

Senator Blair. — Upon what ground did they say, No?

Mr. Jones. — That is what I should like to know. They were not logical. Their answer shows that there is no ground in justice nor in right for their claim that the majority should rule in matters of conscience.

Senator Blair. — That does not follow. At least it does not strike me that it follows. The majority has a right to rule in what pertains to the regulation of society, and if Cæsar regulates society, then the majority has a right in this country to say what we shall render to Cæsar.

Mr. Jones. — Very good, but the majority has no right to say what we shall render *to God ;* nor has it any right to say that we shall render *to Cæsar* that which is *God's.* If nine hundred and ninety-nine out of every one thousand people in the United States kept the seventh day, that is, Saturday, and I deemed it my right, and made it my choice, to keep Sunday, they would have no right to compel me to rest on Saturday.

Senator Blair. — In other words, you take the ground that for the good of society, irrespective of the religious aspect of the question, society may not require abstinence from labor on Sabbath, if it disturbs others?

Mr. Jones. — As to its disturbing others, I have proved that it does not. The body of your question states my position exactly.

Senator Blair. — You are logical all the way through that there shall be no Sabbath. This question was passed me to ask: "Is the speaker also opposed to all laws against blasphemy?"

Mr. Jones. — Yes, sir. But not because **blasphemy** is not wrong, but because civil government **cannot** define blasphemy, nor punish it. Blasphemy pertains to God, it is an offense against him, it is a sin against him.

Senator Blair. — Suppose the practice of it in **society** at large is hurtful to society?

Mr. Jones. — That will have to be explained. How is it hurtful to society?

Senator Blair. — Suppose it be hurtful to society in this way: A belief in the existence of God, and reverence for the Creator, and a cultivation of that sentiment in society, is for the good of society; is, in fact, the basis of all law and restraint. If the Almighty, who knows everything, or is supposed to, and has all power, has no right to restrain us, it is difficult to see how we can restrain each other.

Mr. Jones. — He has the right to restrain us. **He** does restrain us.

Senator Blair. — To commonly blaspheme and deride and ridicule the Almighty, would, of course, have a tendency to bring up the children who are soon **to** be the State, in an absolute disregard of him and his authority. Blasphemy, as I understand it, is that practice which brings the Creator into contempt and **ridicule** among his creatures.

Mr. Jones. — What is blasphemy here, would **not** be blasphemy in China, and many other countries.

Senator Blair. — We are not dealing with **pagan** communities. A regulation that may be appropriate in a pagan community, would not answer men in a Christian community. Do you mean that there is no **such** thing as blasphemy?

Mr. Jones. — No; I do not mean that.

Senator Blair. — The Chinaman hardly believes **in**

any god whatever; at least in no such God as we do. Taking our God and these Christian institutions of ours, what do you understand blasphemy to be?

Mr. Jones. — There are many things that the Scriptures show to be blasphemy.

Senator Blair. — The power of the law has undertaken in various States to say that certain things are blasphemy.

Mr. Jones. — Precisely; but if the law proposes to define blasphemy and punish it, why does it not go to the depth of it, and define all and punish all?

Senator Blair. — Perhaps it may not go as far as it ought. You say you are opposed to all laws against blasphemy, cursing, and swearing?

Mr. Jones. — In relation to any one of the first four commandments.

Senator Palmer. — Suppose that what is defined as blasphemy in the statutes of the several States, should detract from the observance of the law and regard for it, would you regard laws against it as being improper?

Mr. Jones. — Under the principle that the Scripture lays down, no legislation in any way can be proper in regard to the first four commandments. There may be many ways in which it would appear very appropriate for civil government to do this or to do that; but when you have entered upon such legislation, where will you stop?

Senator Palmer. — Abstaining from blasphemy is a part of the education of the youth of the country.

Mr. Jones. — That is true. If youth are properly educated, they will never blaspheme.

Senator Palmer. — We pass laws for the education of the youth. The question is whether abstention from blasphemy could not be included in the scope of education. Take it on that ground.

Mr. Jones. — Idolatry (and covetousness is idolatry) is no more than a violation of the first commandment: "Thou shalt have no other Gods before me;" and if the State can forbid the violation of the third commandment and the fourth, why may it not forbid the violation of the first and the second, and in that case supplant God at once, and establish an earthly theocracy? That is the only logical outcome.

Senator Blair. — Covetousness is a state of mind; but when it becomes practice by stealing — taking from another without consideration — the law interferes.

Mr. Jones. — Certainly.

Senator Palmer. — There is an infection in blasphemy or in covetousness. For instance, if one covetous man in a neighborhood should infuse the whole neighborhood with covetousness to such an extent that all would become thieves, then covetousness would be a proper subject of legislation.

Mr. Jones. — Never! You forbid the theft, not the covetousness. You cannot invade the condition of mind in which lies the covetousness.

Senator Blair. — We do not say that we must invade the condition of mind; but society has a right to make regulations, because those regulations are essential to the good of society. Society by a major vote establishes a regulation, and we have to obey what is settled by the majority.

Mr. Jones. — How shall it be discovered what is blasphemy, as it is only an offense against God? In the Puritan Theocracy of New England, our historian, Bancroft, says that "the highest offense in the catalogue of crimes was blasphemy, or what a jury should call blasphemy."

Senator Blair. — But the law was behind the jury, and said that the practice should be punished. If a jury of twelve men said that one had committed the overt act, then it could be punished. It was the majority who made the law, and the jury only found the question of fact after the law had been violated. The jury did not make the law. This is a question as to making the law.

Mr. Jones. — It is not wholly a question only of making the law. The question is whether the law is right when it is made. There is a limit to the law-making power; and that limit is the line which Jesus Christ has drawn. The government has no right to make any law relating to the things that pertain to God, or offenses against God, or religion. It has nothing to do with religion.

Blasphemy, according to Judge Cooley, in his "Constitutional Limitations," "is purposely using words concerning the Supreme Being, calculated and designed to impair and destroy the reverence, respect, and confidence due to him, as the intelligent Creator, Governor, and Judge of the world; . . . a bad motive must exist; there must be a willful, malicious attempt to lessen men's reverence for the Deity, or for the accepted religion."

It is seen at a glance that this comes from the old English system of statutes regulating "offenses against God and religion." That is where this statute is placed in every system of civil law; it could not be placed anywhere else. But offenses against God are to be answered for only at his tribunal; and with religion, or offenses against it, the civil power has nothing to do. It is a perversion of the functions of civil government to have it made a party to religious controversies. It will have ample exercise for its power and jurisdiction to keep religious disputants as well as other people *civil,* without allowing itself ever to become a partisan in religious disputes and the conservator of religious dogmas.

But according to Judge Cooley's definition, blasphemy is an attempt to lessen men's reverence, not only for the Deity, but for "the accepted religion" as well. But any man in this wide world has the right to lessen men's reverence for the accepted religion, if he thinks that religion to be wrong. Consequently, as I said a moment ago, that which would be counted blasphemy here would not be counted blasphemy in China; and that which is in the strictest accordance with the word of God and the faith of Jesus Christ here, is necessarily blasphemy in China, or in Turkey, or in Russia. A man who preaches the gospel of Jesus Christ in China commits blasphemy under this definition. He does make a willful attempt to lessen men's reverence for their accepted religion, and for the deities recognized in their religion. He has to do so, if he is ever to get them to believe in Christ and the religion of Christ. He has to bring them to the place where they will have no reverence for their deities or for their accepted religion, before they ever can accept the religion of Jesus Christ. It is the same way in Turkey, or any other Mohammedan country, or any heathen country. Wherever the gospel of Jesus Christ is preached in any Mohammedan or heathen country, it is blasphemy under this definition, because its sole object is not only to lessen men's reverence for their deities and for their accepted religion, but to turn them wholly from it, and if possible to obliterate it from their minds.

It is so likewise in Russia. Anybody there who speaks against the accepted religion, or against the saints, or their images, is subject to the penalty of blasphemy, which is banishment for life to Siberia.

3

But if blasphemy be a proper subject of legislation by civil government, if it be right for a government to make itself the "defender of the faith," then it is perfectly proper for the laws of China to prohibit under whatever penalty it pleases, the preaching of the gospel of Jesus Christ within the Chinese dominions; because its effect is to lessen men's reverence for the deities recognized by China, and for the accepted religion of the country. It is the same way in any of the other countries named. And in that case there is no such thing as persecution on account of religion. The only persecutions that have ever been, were because of men's speaking against the accepted religion. If this principle be correct, then the Roman empire did perfectly right in prohibiting under penalty of death the preaching of the religion of Jesus Christ. Whenever Paul, or any of his brethren, spoke in the Roman empire, they blasphemed according to the Roman law. They were held as blasphemers, and were put to death under the very principle of this definition, which is the principle of the American statutes on the subject of blasphemy. The Christians had to tell the Roman empire that the Roman gods were no gods. They had to tell the Roman empire that the genius of Rome itself, which the Roman system held to be the supreme deity, was not such; but that it was subordinate, and that there was a higher idea of God and of right than the Roman empire or the Roman law knew anything of. They did speak deliberately against the chief deity of Rome, and all the gods of Rome. They did it with the express purpose of destroying reverence for them and for the accepted religion. Rome put them to death. And I repeat, if the principle of the American statutes against blasphemy is correct, then Rome did right.

To make this clearer, I quote a passage from the Supreme Court of Pennsylvania in defense of this principle, in a decision upon this very subject, which says: "To prohibit the open, public, and explicit denial of the popular religion of a country, is a necessary measure to preserve the tranquillity of a government." That is precisely what the Roman empire did. Christianity did openly, publicly, and explicitly deny the popular religion of the country. It did it with intent to destroy men's reverence for the deities and the religion of that country. Rome prohibited it; and upon the principle of the decision of the Supreme Court of Pennsylvania, which is the principle of American law on blasphemy, Rome did right, and Christianity was a blaspheming religion. The principle of this decision seems to be that those who represent the popular religion of a country have so little of the real virtue of the religion which they profess, that if anybody speaks against it, it is sure to rouse their combativeness to such a degree as to endanger the public tranquillity. Therefore, in order to keep civil those who represent the popular religion, the State must forbid anybody to deny that religion.

This decision of the Supreme Court of Pennsylvania is one of the grand precedents that have been followed in all the later decisions upon this subject in the younger States; but this decision itself followed one by Chief Justice Kent of the Supreme Court of New York in 1811, in which he embodies the same principles. He defends the right of the State to punish such offenses against what he calls a Christian people, and not equally to punish like offenses against the religion of other people in this country, by the following argument: —

"Nor are we bound by any expressions in the Constitution, as some have strangely supposed, either not to punish at all, or to punish indiscriminately the like attacks upon the religion of Mohammed, or of the Grand Llama, and for this plain reason : that the case assumes that we are a Christian people, and the morality of the country is deeply engrafted upon Christianity, and not upon the doctrines or worship of those impostors."

This is only to argue that if the morality of the country were engrafted upon the religion of Mohammed or the Grand Llama, and Christians were to speak against and deny that accepted religion, it would be proper that the State should punish those Christians for so doing. If that principle be correct, then a Mohammedan country has the right to prohibit the preaching of the gospel of Jesus Christ within its limits.

According to these decisions, Luther and the reformers of his day were blasphemers. The penalty was death, in many cases at the stake, yet under this principle the State did right to put them to death in whatever way the law prescribed ; because they did certainly make an open, public, and explicit denial of the popular religion of every country in which they lived, and of all Europe ; and if the words of Luther were used to-day in any Catholic country, they would be counted as blasphemous, as a willful and malicious reviling of the accepted religion. The reformers did hold up to ridicule and contempt the popular religion of all Europe. They did right, too ; and when the State punished them, it was but carrying out the principles upheld by Chancellor Kent and the Supreme Court of Pennsylvania, and all the other States that have legislated on the subject of religion.

As I have already stated, it was upon this principle precisely that the Roman empire forbade the preaching of the gospel of Christ. It only forbade an open, public, and explicit denial of the popular religion of the country, yet in forbidding that, it forbade the preaching of the gospel of Christ. But Christ sent forth his disciples to preach the gospel to every creature, and they did it in the face of the Roman law, and in opposition to the whole power of the Roman empire ; and everybody in all the world has an undeniable right to make an open, public, and explicit denial of the popular religion of this country, or any other, if he thinks that religion to be wrong.

The principle of these decisions and of the civil statutes against blasphemy, is essentially a pagan principle, and not a Christian principle. It is peculiarly appropriate, therefore, that Chief Justice Kent not only cited the precedents of the church-and-state principles of the colonies and of the British government, but appealed to the pagan governments of antiquity and the papal institutions of modern Europe, as the basis of his decision. It is true that all these nations have set themselves up as the special guardians of their deities, and have prohibited the denial of the popular religion ; and it is equally true that all these nations have resisted every step in enlightenment and progress that has ever been made in the march of time. Every step forward in religion and in enlightenment has of necessity been taken in the face of all the opposition which these States and empires could bring to bear. But the principles of American institutions are neither pagan nor papal. The principles of the American Constitution which forbids legislation on the subject of religion, are Christian principles. And it is strictly in order for Supreme Courts in making decisions in behalf of what they boast of as the Christian religion, to base their decision upon something else than the course of the pagan governments of antiquity, and the papal institutions of modern Europe. Upon such a subject it would seem to be proper for them to refer to the teachings and the principles of the Author of Christianity, but singularly enough, it has never been done, and doubtless for the very good reason that it never can be done ; for the teachings of Jesus Christ are directly against it. His word forbids civil government to have anything to do with what pertains to God. And instead of teaching his disciples to prosecute, to fine, and to punish by civil law those who speak against them or their religion, he says, " Love your enemies, do good to them that hate you, pray for them that despitefully use you and persecute you ; that ye may be the children of your Father which is in heaven." How can men be brought to respect God or Jesus Christ by civil penalties upon their bodies and goods? How can they respect the religion of men who are ready to prosecute and imprison them? Every principle of the thing is contrary both to the spirit and the letter of Christianity. The religion of Jesus Christ properly exemplified in the daily lives of those who profess it, is the best argument and the strongest defense against blasphemy, both as defined by the Scriptures and by the civil statutes.

Laws, therefore, prohibiting " what a jury may call blasphemy," are pagan, and not Christian. The decisions of the Supreme Courts of New York and Pennsylvania upon this subject are pagan decisions, and not Christian ; they are based upon pagan precedents, not Christian. The deadly persecutions of all history, pagan, papal, and so-called Protestant, are justified in these decisions. Michael Servetus was burnt for " blasphemy." The only use that ever has been, or ever is, made of any such laws in any country, is to give some

religious bigots who profess the popular religion, an opportunity to vent their wrath upon persons who disagree
with them.   Any man who really possesses the religion
of Christ will have enough of the grace of God to keep
him from endangering the public tranquillity when his
religion is spoken against.

Therefore, I say that we are opposed to all laws of
civil government against blasphemy, not because blasphemy is not wrong, but because it is a wrong of that
kind with which civil government has nothing to do ;
and in this we stand wholly upon Christian principle.
We stand exactly where the early Christians stood ;
for, I say again, when Paul spoke in the Roman empire,
he was blaspheming, according to the law, was held
as a blasphemer and an atheist, and was put to death
as such, under the very principle upon which the American laws of blasphemy are sustained.

Senator Blair. — The law was wrong, you say ?

Mr. Jones. — Certainly the law was wrong.   The
Roman law was that no man should have particular
gods of his own, — gods not recognized by the Roman
law.

Senator Blair. — That law was not for the good of
society ?

Mr. Jones. — No, sir.

Senator Blair. — Certainly it was not.   Then you
have to repeal the law or obey it.

Mr. Jones. — It ought to be repealed.

Senator Blair. — During these eighteen hundred
years we have contrived to repeal that law ; but here
comes an intelligent people who have evolved among
themselves, as the result of a thousand or fifteen hundred years of history, among other things, the institution of the Christian Sabbath, by writing it in the

laws of every State in this country, so that the whole American people made up of communities or States, have enacted the principle of this law.

Mr. Jones. — The same principle is under the bill before the Committee. There is the same principle under it all. If you can legislate in regard to the Sabbath, you can legislate in regard to blasphemy; you can legislate in regard to idolatry, and every other offense against God, as did both the Puritan and the papal theocracy.

Senator Blair. — You deny the right of the majority, in other words, to make a law in conformity with which the whole shall practice in society?

Mr. Jones. — I deny the right of any civil government to make any law respecting anything that pertains to man's relationship to his God, under the first four of the ten commandments. I wish right here to show further that this is not only the principle of the word of Jesus Christ, but also of the American Constitution.

Before Christianity was preached in the world, the Roman empire had among its laws these statutes: —

" 1. No man shall have for himself particular gods of his own ; no man shall worship by himself any new or foreign gods, unless they are recognized by the public laws.

" 2. Worship the gods in all respects according to the laws of your country, and compel all others to do the same. But hate and punish those who would introduce anything whatever alien to our customs in this particular.

" 3. Whoever introduces new religions, the tendency and character of which are unknown, whereby the minds of men may be disturbed, shall, if belonging to the higher rank, be banished ; if to the lower, punished with death."

The Christians did have a particular God of their own, not recognized by the Roman law. They did introduce a new religion. The Roman empire enforced the law, and that is why the Christians were put to death. If things pertaining to God be a proper subject of legislation by civil government, then no Christian was ever persecuted, and there has never been persecution in this world. All the Roman empire did in killing Christians was to enforce the law. Then the question was with the Christians, at that time, and the question is with us, Is not the law wrong? and did not the Christians have the right to attack the law? That is what they did. When a Christian was brought before the magistrate, a dialogue followed something like this : —

Magistrate. — "Have you a particular God of your own, — a god not recognized by the Roman law?"

Christian. — "Yes."

M. — "Did you not know that the law is against it?"

C. — "Yes."

M. — "Have you not introduced a new religion?"

C. — "Yes."

M. — "Did you not know that the law is against it?"

C. — "Yes."

M. — "Did you not know that the penalty is death, for those of the lower ranks?"

C. — "Yes."

M. — "You are of the lower ranks?"

C. — "Yes."

M. — "You have introduced a new religion?"

C. — "Yes."

M. — "You have a God of your own?"

C. — "Yes."

M. — "What is the penalty?"

C. — "Death."

That was all. The Romans enforced the law upon the Christians in the first days of Christianity ; and there was no persecution in it, if the principle be recognized that civil government has a right to legislate in religious things. The empire had this apparent advantage, too, that the law existed before Christianity was known in the world. Christianity appeared to Rome as nothing else than an uprising against the imperial power. Laws are made to be enforced; and to enforce the law is all that the Roman empire ever did, whether up to the time of Constantine, or at any other time. In fact, all the papacy did in the Middle Ages was to have the emperors enforce the law. We stand to-day just where the Christians did at that time; we come to the root of the whole matter, and deny the right of the civil government to legislate on anything that pertains to our duties to God under the first four commandments, and assert the Christian and American principle that every man has the right to worship God according to the dictates of his own conscience.

The principle that the Christians asserted was to render to Cæsar that which is Cæsar's, and to deny the right of Cæsar to demand anything that pertains to God. They gave their lives in support of that principle, against the law of the Roman empire, and against the very existence of the Roman empire. This principle was asserted and maintained until it forced the Roman empire, with all its power, to recognize the right of every man to have a particular god of his own, and to worship that god as he chose. The Roman empire did come in the days of Constantine and Licinius to that point. At the death of Galerius, it was decreed in the Roman law, by the emperors Constantine and Licinius in the Edict of Milan, that every man should be at liberty to have any god he pleased, and worship him as he pleased. But it was the Christian principle that forced the Roman empire to that point in the face of all its laws and institutions of ages.

Our national Constitution embodies the very principle announced by Jesus Christ, that the civil government shall have nothing to do with religion, or with what pertains to God ; but shall leave that to every man's conscience and his God. As long as he is a good citizen, the nation will protect him and leave him perfectly free to worship whom he pleases, when he pleases, as he pleases, or not to worship at all, if he pleases.

In Article VI. of the Constitution of the United States, this nation says that "no religious test shall ever be required as a qualification to any office or public trust under the United States." By an amendment making more certain the adoption of the principle, it declares in the first amendment to the Constitution, "Congress shall make no law respecting an establishment of religion, or prohibiting the free exercise thereof." This first amendment was adopted in 1789, by the first Congress that ever met under the Constitution. In 1796 a treaty was made with Tripoli, in which it was declared (Article II.) that "the Government of the United States of America is not in any sense founded on the Christian religion." This treaty was framed by an ex-Congregationalist clergyman, and was signed by President Washington. It was not out of disrespect to religion or Christianity that these clauses were placed in the Constitution, and that this one was inserted in that treaty. On the contrary, it was entirely on account of their respect for religion, and the Christian religion in particular, as being beyond the province of civil government, pertaining solely to the conscience, and resting entirely between the individual and God. This fact is so well stated by Mr. Bancroft in his "History of the Constitution of the United States," that I will here insert it : —

"In the earliest States known to history, government and religion were one and indivisible. Each State had its special deity, and often these protectors, one after another, might be overthrown in battle, never to rise again. The Peloponnesian War grew out of a strife about an oracle. Rome, as it sometimes adopted into citizenship those whom it vanquished, introduced in like manner, and with good logic for that day, the worship of their gods. No one thought of vindicating religion for the conscience of the individual, till a voice in Judea, breaking day for the greatest epoch in the life of humanity, by establishing a pure, spiritual, and universal religion for all mankind, enjoined to render to Cæsar only that which is Cæsar's. The rule was upheld during the infancy of the gospel for all men. No sooner was this religion adopted by the chief of the Roman empire, than it was shorn of its character of universality, and enthralled by an unholy connection with the unholy State ; and so it continued till the new nation, — the least defiled with the barren scoffings of the eighteenth century, the most general believer in Christianity of any people of that age, the chief heir of the Reformation in its purest forms, — when it came to establish a government for the United States, refused to treat faith as a matter to be regulated by a corporate body, or having a headship in a monarch or a State.

"Vindicating the right of individuality even in religion, and in religion above all, *the new nation dared to set the example of accepting in its relations to God the principle first divinely ordained of God in Judea.* It left the management of temporal things to the temporal power ; but the American Constitution, in harmony with the people of the several States, withheld from the Federal Government the power to invade the home of reason, the citadel of conscience, the sanctuary of the soul ; and not from indifference, but that the infinite Spirit of eternal truth might move in its freedom and purity and power."— *Last chapter.*

At this point I am brought to the assertion of the second of the principles upon which we stand in our opposition to Sunday laws, or any other form of religious legislation : that is, the principle of the Constitution of the United States ; and upon this principle I maintain that this proposed Sunday law *is unconstitutional.*

The object of this Sunday bill is wholly religious. The last section shows the object of the entire bill ; and that is, "to secure to the whole people rest, . . . and the religious observance of the Sabbath day." No one, therefore, need attempt to evade the force of objections against this bill by saying that it is not the religious, but the *civil,* observance of the day that is required ; because it is plainly declared in the bill itself, that it is not only to secure rest to all the people, but that it is also to secure the *religious* observance of the Sabbath day. There is not a single reference in the bill to any such thing as the civil observance of the day. The word *civil* is not used in the bill. It is a religious bill wholly. The title of the bill declares that its object is to secure to the people the enjoyment of the Lord's day as a day of rest, "and to promote its observance as a day of *religious worship.*" The first section defines the Lord's day ; the second section refers to the day as one of worship and rest ; the third section refers to it as a day of religious worship ; the fourth section refers to its observance as that of religious worship ; and the sixth section plainly declares, what is apparent throughout, that the object of the bill is "to secure to the whole people rest, . . . and the *religious* observance of the Sabbath day," on the first day of the week.

It is the religious observance of the day that its promoters, from one end of the land to the other, have in view. In the convention, now in session in this city, working in behalf of this bill, only yesterday Dr. Crafts said : —

"Taking religion out of the day, takes the rest out."

In the "Boston Monday Lectures," 1887, Joseph Cook, lecturing on the subject of Sunday laws, said : —

"The experience of centuries shows, however, that you will in vain endeavor to preserve Sunday as a day of rest, unless you preserve it as a day of worship. Unless Sabbath observance be *founded upon religious reasons*, you will not long maintain it at a high standard on the basis of economic and physiological and political considerations only."

And in the Illinois State Sunday convention held in Elgin, Nov. 8. 1887, Dr. W. W. Everts declared Sunday to be "the test of all religion."

Sunday is a religious institution wholly ; Sunday legislation, wherever found, is religious legislation solely ; and this bill does not in its terms pretend to be anything else than religious. Being therefore as it is, religious legislation, it is clearly unconstitutional. In proof of this, I submit the following considerations : —

All the powers of Congress are delegated powers. It has no other power ; it cannot exercise any other. Article X. of Amendments to the Constitution expressly declares that —

"The powers not delegated to the United States by the Constitution, or prohibited by it to the States, are reserved to the States respectively, or to the people."

In all the powers thus delegated to Congress, there is no hint of any power to legislate upon any religious question, or in regard to the observance of any religious institution or rite. Therefore, this Sunday bill, being a religious bill, is unconstitutional ; and any legislation with regard to it will be unconstitutional. Sunday being a religious institution, any legislation by Congress in regard to its observance, will be unconstitutional as long as the United States Constitution shall remain as it now is.

Nor is this all. The nation has not been left in doubt as to whether the failure to delegate this power was or was not intentional. The first amendment to the Constitution, in declaring that "Congress shall make no law respecting an establishment of religion, or prohibiting the free exercise thereof," shows that the failure to delegate such power was intentional, and makes the intention emphatic by absolutely prohibiting Congress from exercising any power with regard to religion. It is impossible to frame a law on the subject of religion that will not prohibit the free exercise of religion. Therefore the first amendment to the Constitution absolutely prohibits Congress from ever making any law with regard to any religious subject, or the observance of any religious rite or institution.

More than this, the National Reform Association knows, and has been contending for twenty-five years, that for Congress to make any Sunday laws would be unconstitutional. Yet the National Reform Association is one of the most prominent agencies in urging forward this bill; and the Secretary of that Association stood at this table to-day to plead for its passage. And this only shows that they are willing knowingly to resort to unconstitutional means to secure their coveted power, and to accomplish their purposes. As for Dr. Crafts and his fellow-workers, whether or not they know it to be unconstitutional, we do not know. In the announcements of the national Sunday-law convention now (Dec. 11–13, 1888) being held in this city, it was stated that the church in which the convention was to meet would

be festooned with the names of six millions of petitioners ; but at the beginning of the first meeting it was
stated that there were *fourteen* millions of them.   A
question was sent up asking how the number could have
grown so much larger so suddenly.   Mrs. Bateham was
recalled to the platform to answer the question, and
when she answered it, the cause of such a sudden and
enormous growth was explained by the fact that Cardinal Gibbons had written a letter indorsing the bill,
and solely upon the strength of his name, seven million
two hundred thousand Catholics were counted as *petitioners.*

This was not a complete answer to the question, because the Cardinal's letter does not authorize any such
use of it as they have made, at least so much of it as
was made public does not.   The whole of the letter was
not made public there, because, Dr. Crafts' said, it was
for the Senate Committee.   It was laid on the table
here to-day.   But so much of it as was read merely referred to the action of the Baltimore Council in commanding a stricter observance of Sunday, and said : —

"I am most happy to add my name to those of the
millions of others who are laudably contending against
the violation of the Christian Sabbath by unnecessary
labor, and who are endeavoring to promote its decent
and proper observance by judicious legislation."

This was all.   He said, "I am happy to add *my
name,*" etc.   He did not say that he added, or that he
wished to add, seven million two hundred thousand
others with his name, or in his name ; yet this was done.
But it was not so much to be wondered at, because
the same principle had been acted upon before throughout the country, and when five hundred petitioners
could be made out of *one* hundred, and two hundred

and forty *thousand* out of two hundred and forty, it was perfectly easy and entirely consistent to make seven million two hundred thousand and one out of *one*.

This thing was perfectly consistent also with the principle in another point. The petition reads : "We, the undersigned, *adult* residents of the United States, *twenty-one years of age or more*, hereby petition," etc. In counting these seven million two hundred thousand petitioners in behalf of the Sunday law, they thereby certified that all these were Catholics "twenty-one years of age or more." But there was not a man in that convention, and there is not a woman in the Woman's Christian Temperance Union, who does not know that there are not that many Catholics in the United States "twenty-one years of age or more." They virtually certified that all the Catholics in the United States are "twenty-one years of age or more," for they distinctly announced that "all the Roman Catholics" were petitioning for the Sunday law. But as they had virtually certified the same thing of the Protestant churches throughout the country, why should they not go on and swing in "all the Roman Catholics" in the same way? They could do the one just as honestly as they could do the other. When men and women professing themselves to be Protestant Christians will do such things as that to carry the Catholic Church with them, it is not to be wondered at if they should be willing to resort to unconstitutional means to make their religious zeal effective in national law.

Senator Blair. — Then you assume that this bill and all Sunday laws concern only the relation of man to God, and not the relation of men to each other?

Mr. Jones. — Yes, sir, that is the principle upon which we stand.

Senator Blair. — Right there I find fault with your original proposition. You have got to establish, before you can defeat the ground of Sunday laws, that Sunday laws are not for the good of Cæsar ; that is, not for the good of society.

Mr. Jones. — I have not had time to prove that yet. I will prove fully that Sunday laws are not for the good of anybody.

Senator Blair. — Come to the point as soon as you can. That is the point in this case, as between you and the law proposed to be enacted.

Mr. Jones. — Very good. For the State to compel men to do no work is to enforce idleness. Idleness is the root of unlimited evil. It is a true proverb that we learned in our boyhood, "Satan always finds something for idle hands to do." In this world, to compel men to be idle is to force them into a line of influences and temptations which in the very nature of things can end only in evil. It is well known, and it is one of the principal grounds of the complaints of those who are working for Sunday laws, that Sunday is, of all the week, the day of the most wickedness ; that the record of crime and violence on Sunday exceeds that of any other day of the week, especially in large cities.

Dr. Crafts refers constantly to London as an exemplary city in the matter of enforced Sunday laws, but the fact was brought out last spring by a member of this Committee — Senator Payne — that the statement had lately been "made on authority, that London on Sunday is the most immoral and dissipated city in the world." Now why is this? They argue that it is because the saloons are open on Sunday. But the saloons are open every other day of the week. Then the saloons being open no more on Sunday than on any

other day, why is it that there is so much more violence
done on Sunday than on other days of the week? — It
is because more men are idle on Sunday than on any
other day of the week. Upon this point I quote an
extract from the *Cincinnati Commercial Gazette* of
March 10, 1888.

"They declare Sunday the moral ruin of the people.
They prove it by alleged statistics of criminal prosecutions to show that more crimes of violence are committed on Sunday than on all other days of the week.
Why is this? Because the saloons are open? — They
are open on other days. This reduces them to the sole
reason that it is because it is a day of idleness.
"Their argument is absolutely destructive to the
beneficence of the custom of a rest day. They continually affirm that a Sabbath day is the very foundation of religion, morals, and society, and they as
incessantly declare that the custom of Sunday cessation from work in the cities had made it a day of moral
ruin. What is their recourse from the destruction which
they charge upon the day of idleness? — *To make statutes more stringent to enforce idleness.* Arguing that
idleness on that day leads mankind to moral ruin, they
call for a more rigid enforcement of idleness, to lead
mankind to the ways of salvation.
"Surely there is need to revise their basis in season
before they can proceed rationally in legislation. Selling beer is no more a sin on Sunday than on other
days. The reason why more crimes of violence are
done on Sunday than on other days — if that is a fact
— is not that the saloons are open, but that the men
are idle. The good of a day of rest for the toilers has
to be taken with the drawback of this unavoidable evil
from idleness and indulgences of appetites. The *cause*
is the *cessation of vocations.*"

This argument is entirely sound. We submit to the
consideration of any candid mind that it would be far
better to allow men to follow their honest occupations

on Sunday as they do on other days of the week, than to compel them to be idle, and thus forcibly throw them into the way of all the temptations and evil that beset men in this world. No State, therefore, can ever afford for its own good to enact laws making idleness compulsory, as Sunday laws do.

More than this, to prohibit men from following their honest occupations at any time, under penalties of fine or imprisonment, or perhaps both, is for the State to relegate honest occupations to the realm of crime, and put a premium upon idleness and recklessness. It is well known that in many localities if a man will only be idle on Sunday, he can run into all sorts of dissipation and wickedness to any extent, except that of down-right violence, without any fear of prosecution or penalty of any kind. But if any quiet, industrious citizen chooses to engage in his honest occupation, — going quietly about his own business on his own premises on Sunday, — he is subjected to prosecution, to a penalty of a heavy fine, and perhaps imprisonment. This is nothing else than to put a premium upon wickedness. No State can afford to make crimes of honest occupations. No State can afford to put such a premium upon idleness and all its attendant wickedness.

All these complaints of evil and violence and wickedness on Sunday, so enlarged upon by the people who are working for Sunday laws, is an open confession that wickedness is the effect of enforced idleness, and this in itself is the strongest argument that can be offered against the very things for which they plead. The States of the Union have all these years been sowing the wind in this very thing, and now they are reaping the whirlwind. And, worse than all, they propose to cure the evils of all this enforced idleness by more stringently enforcing more idleness throughout the whole nation, and by the national power.

It may be answered that this reflects upon the wisdom of God in appointing a day of rest; but it does not. God appointed the Sabbath for a purpose; and that purpose is that men should remember him in his works of creation, and worship him as Creator.

The intention of the commandment enjoining the observance of the Sabbath day, is the honor of God, and his worship as Creator. This worship and the religious sanctions which God has associated with the Sabbath, are considerations which will ever prevent the day from becoming a day of idleness to those who keep the Sabbath in obedience to him; and the worship of God and the religious sanctions which he has put upon the Sabbath, are the only things that ever can prevent the Sabbath from becoming a day of idleness. Those who advocate this Sunday bill well know this. This whole principle is embodied in that statement Dr. Crafts made to the Knights of Labor, that " if you take *religion* out of the day, you take the *rest* out." The same principle is also apparent in the words of Joseph Cook, before referred to, that you will in vain endeavor to secure the enforcement of a day of rest unless you enforce it as *a day of worship;* and unless it be founded on *religious* reasons, it cannot be long maintained.

Thus these men themselves confess the point which I here make: that it is only the religious sanctions and worship that can ever keep a day of rest from being a day of idleness, and of consequent wickedness. But *it is only God* who can furnish those sanctions; *the State never can.* Therefore, the next step in the proceeding on the part of those who are calling for this law is to have the State attempt to supply the religious sanctions which belong with the day of rest, and which only can keep it from being a day of idleness and a day of evil. But they know that the State has none of those religious sanctions; and they know that these will have to be supplied to the State by the church, and then the church will call upon the State, by its power, to force them upon the citizen.

This is precisely what is proposed. Rev. Sam Small, in a sermon in Kansas City last winter, expressed the views of many more than himself, when he said : —

"I want to see the day come when the church shall be the arbiter of all legislation, State, national, and municipal ; when the great churches of the country can come together harmoniously, and issue their edict, and the legislative powers will respect it, and enact it into laws."

But any attempt to enforce religious observances only enforces hypocrisy and multiplies sin, because love for God is essential to every act of religious duty. For a man to tender obedience or homage to God when he has no love for God in his heart, only dishonors God, and does violence to his own nature. For anybody to obey God, or perform religious observances from interested motives, is sin ; and for the State to exert its power in compelling men to act religiously, and pretend to honor God when they have in the heart no love for God, is only to force them into hypocrisy, and to compel them to commit sin, which, increased and multiplied by the exertion of national power, can end only in ruin, and that speedily.

For as Mr. Buckle has most forcibly expressed it : —

" In this way, men being constrained to mask their thoughts, there arises a habit ʻof securing safety by falsehood, and of purchasing impunity with deceit. In this way, fraud becomes a necessity of life ; insincerity is made a daily custom ; the whole tone of public feeling is vitiated ; and the gross amount of vice and of error fearfully increased."

Consequently, it is only at its own peril that the State can ever enforce the observance of a day of rest.

More than this, for the State to allow itself to be dictated to by the church as is here proposed by Mr. Small, is to render the church superior to the civil power, which can end in nothing but a religious despotism, which is the worst of all despotisms. Thus by every line of reasoning that can spring from the subject, it is demonstrated that for the State to fix a day of compulsory rest can only end in evil. Therefore, my proposition is proved, that Sunday laws are not for the good of anybody.

Further : as it is only the religious sanctions which surround a day of rest, that can prevent it from being a day of idleness, and consequently of evil ; and as God only can supply these sanctions, it follows that to God only, can Sabbath observance be rendered. He only can command it ; he only can secure it ; and being a duty which can be rendered only to God, we are brought again directly to the command of Jesus Christ, to render unto God, not to Cæsar, that which is God's, which clearly forbids the State to have anything to do with Sabbath observance.

This whole line of argument is fully sustained by the Sabbath commandment itself. That commandment says : "Remember the Sabbath day, to keep it holy. Six days shalt thou labor, and do all thy work : but the seventh day is the Sabbath of the Lord thy God : in it

thou shalt not do any work, thou, nor thy son, nor thy
daughter, thy man-servant, nor thy maid-servant, nor
thy cattle, nor thy stranger that is within thy gates:
for in six days the Lord made heaven and earth, the
sea, and all that in them is, and rested the seventh day:
wherefore the Lord blessed the Sabbath day, and hallowed it."

Here are the reasons: first, he rested on the seventh
day; second, he blessed it and made it holy. That you
may become tired is not given as a reason for doing no
work on the seventh day. God does not say that on the
seventh day you shall do no work, because if you should,
you would overdo or break down your physical system.
Nothing of the kind. Man's physical wants are not referred to in the commandment. It says, Work six days,
because *the Lord* worked six days; rest on the seventh
day, because *the Lord* rested on the seventh day; keep
that day holy, because the Lord blessed it and made it
holy. It is the Lord who is to be held in view. It is
the Lord who is to be exalted. Therefore the fourth
commandment and its obligations have solely to do with
man's relationship to God. It is not man's *physical*, but
his *spiritual*, needs that are held in view in the Sabbath
commandment. It is intended to be a day in which to
worship God, — a day of holy remembrance of him, and
of meditation upon his works. The day is to be kept *holy*.
If it is not kept holy, it is not kept at all. When the
State undertakes to demand the observance of the Sabbath, or Lord's day, it demands of men that which does
not belong to it, but which belongs only to God. When
the State undertakes to secure the observance of the
Sabbath, it undertakes that which, to it, is an impossible task, because holiness is not an attribute of civil
government, nor has it either the power or the creden-

tials to promote holiness ; and as has been already demonstrated, all that it ever can do in any such effort is to enforce idleness and put a premium upon recklessness, which, for its own welfare, the State can never afford to do. If the State undertakes to supply, from whatever source, the religious sanctions which alone can keep the day from being one of idleness, generating evil, it only enforces hypocrisy, and increases sin.

Therefore I repeat, that by every logical consideration of the subject, I have sustained my proposition that Sunday laws are not for the good of anybody or anything in this world.

Senator Blair. — Do you understand that this bill undertakes to make anybody worship God ?

Mr. Jones. — Yes, sir, I affirm that it does ; and I will prove it by statements made by those who stood here to-day. But I have some other points to make first ; and here I propose to introduce my historical argument. I want you all to see that in this way the papacy was made in the fourth century. I shall read all that I do read, perhaps, on this point, from Neander's Church History, vol. 2, Prof. Torrey's edition, Boston, 1852. I can only refer to it by the page. As I have related, the Roman empire was forced by the principles of Christ, to recognize the right of every man to worship as he chose. This right was recognized in the Edict of Milan, A. D. 312. But liberty of conscience trembled in the balance but a moment, and then the bishopric, with that ambitious spirit that developed the papacy, took up the strain, and carried forward that line of work which ended in the imperious despotism of the Middle Ages. I want you to see just how that was done, and you will then have no difficulty in seeing the tendency of the present movement.

Neander says : —

" There had in fact arisen in the church a false theocratical theory, originating not in the essence of the
gospel, but in the confusion of the religious constitutions of the Old and New Testaments, which . . .
brought along with it an unchristian opposition of the
spiritual to the secular power, and which might easily
result in the formation of a sacerdotal State, subor-
dinating the secular to itself in a false and outward
way."— p. 132.

A theocratical theory of government tending to
subordinate the secular to itself, was the scheme. In
other words, the church aimed to make the ecclesiastical power superior to the civil power. These theocratical bishops made themselves and their power a
necessity to Constantine, who, in order to make sure
of their support, became a political convert to the form
of Christianity, and made it the recognized religion of
the empire ; for says Neander further : —

" This theocratical theory was already the prevailing
one in the time of Constantine ; and . . . the bishops
voluntarily made themselves dependent on him by
their disputes, and by their determination to make use
of the power of the State for the furtherance of their
aims." — *Idem.*

Out of that theocratical theory of government came
the papacy, which did subordinate the civil to the
ecclesiastical power, and that same spirit is to be
guarded against to-day in the United States as much
as in any other country.

I want you to see that there is a theocratical
theory underlying this whole scheme. Mrs. Bateham
has said that the Woman's Christian Temperance
Union started this movement a short time ago, and
that they had worked it up. What is their aim in civil

government? I quote from the monthly reading of the Woman's Christian Temperance Union of September, 1886, — a monthly reading for all the local Unions throughout the country — the following : —

"A true theocracy is yet to come, and the enthronement of Christ in law and law-makers ; hence I pray devoutly, as a Christian patriot, for the ballot in the hands of women, and rejoice that the National Woman's Christian Temperance Union has so long championed this cause."

A theocratical theory, you see, is behind this movement, and is again coming in to interefere in civil things, to establish a theocracy, and to subordinate the civil power at last, to the ecclesiastical.

Senator Blair. — Do you think that the question of giving the ballot to women is a religious question ?

Mr. Jones. — No. I only read this for the purpose of giving the proof that there is a theocratical theory underlying this, as there was that in the fourth century, so as to show the parallel.

Senator Blair. — But the parallel seems to imply that the extension of the suffrage to woman is by divine appointment, and is the introduction of a theocratic form of government ?

Mr. Jones. — Yes, they want the ballot so as to make a theocracy successful.

Senator Blair. — Therefore you would be against woman's suffrage ?

Mr. Jones. — I would be against woman's suffrage, or any other kind of suffrage, to establish a theocracy.

Senator Blair. — But that is not the question. It is possible these women have misstated their own idea there.

Mr. Jones. — No, because I have other proofs. Let me read them.

Senator Palmer. — Do you suppose they intended there a practical theocracy?

Mr. Jones. — I do, sir; but let me read further, and you will get their own words.

Senator Blair. — If these women are trying to overthrow the institutions of the country, and are about to establish a sacerdotal State, we ought to know it.

Mr. Jones. — That is true, and that is why I am speaking here; we want the nation to know it.

Senator Blair. — These women need looking after, I admit.

Mr. Jones. — They do in that respect, and there are many men concerned in the same business.

Senator Blair. — Otherwise it would not be dangerous.

Mr. Jones. — It would be dangerous anyway. A theocratical theory of government is dangerous anywhere. It is antichristian, as well as contrary to right and the principles of justice.

Senator Blair. — Do you suppose that the government of heaven is a theocracy?

Mr. Jones. — Yes, sir; but a civil government — a government of earth — is not.

Senator Blair. — Then why is it dangerous?

Mr. Jones. — Governments of earth are not dangerous when properly controlled.

Senator Blair. — They only say that a true theocracy is yet to come. A millennium is supposed to be coming; perhaps they have reference to a millennium that we have not yet got, so that they will wait some years before they get it.

Mr. Jones. — But I am going to read what kind of laws they propose to make to bring in the millennium.

Senator Blair. — So far as you have read, you have not touched the question; for they say a true theocracy is yet to come, and it may be they are looking to the coming down of the New Jerusalem, for the time of the new theocracy.

Mr. Jones. — No, because no true theocracy can ever come through civil laws, or through politics, or through the ballot.

Senator Blair. — That is not sure at all.

Mr. Jones. — It is by the Scriptures.

Senator Blair. — I do not know; I have read the Bible several times. But go on.

Mr. Jones. — The government of Israel was a true theocracy. That was really a government of God. At the burning bush, God commissioned Moses to lead his people out of Egypt. By signs and wonders and mighty miracles multiplied, God delivered Israel from Egypt, and led them through the wilderness, and finally into the promised land. There he ruled them by judges "until Samuel the prophet," to whom, when he was a child, God spoke, and by whom he made known his will. In the days of Samuel, the people asked that they might have a king. This was allowed, and God chose Saul, and Samuel anointed him king of Israel. Saul failed to do the will of God, and as he rejected the word of the Lord, the Lord rejected him from being king, and sent Samuel to anoint David king of Israel ; and David's throne God established forevermore. When Solomon succeeded to the kingdom in the place of David his father, the record is : " Then Solomon sat on the *throne of the Lord* as king instead of David his father." 1 Chron. 29 : 23. David's throne was the throne of the Lord, and Solomon sat on the throne of the Lord as king over the earthly kingdom of God. The succession to the throne descended in David's line to Zedekiah, who was made subject to the king of Babylon, and who entered into a solemn covenant before God that he

would loyally render allegiance to the king of Babylon. But Zedekiah broke his covenant; and then God
said to him : —

"Thou profane, wicked prince of Israel, whose day
is come, when iniquity shall have an end, thus saith
the Lord God; Remove the diadem, and take off the
crown: this shall not be the same: exalt him that is
low, and abase him that is high. I will overturn,
overturn, overturn it, and it shall be no more, until he
come whose right it is; and I will give it him." Eze.
21 : 25–27 ; see chap. 17 : 1–21.

The kingdom was then subject to Babylon. When
Babylon fell, and Medo-Persia succeeded, it was overturned the first time. When Medo-Persia fell, and was
succeeded by Grecia, it was overturned the second time.
When the Greek empire gave way to Rome, it was
overturned the third time. And then says the word,
"It shall be no more, until he come whose right it is;
and I will give it him." Who is he whose right it is?—
"Thou . . . shalt call his name Jesus. He shall be
great, and shall be called the Son of the Highest; and
the Lord God shall give unto him the throne of his
father David; and he shall reign over the house of
Jacob forever; and of his kingdom there shall be no
end." Luke 1 : 31–33. And while he was here as "that
prophet," a man of sorrows and acquainted with grief,
the night in which he was betrayed he himself declared,
"My kingdom is not of this world." Thus the throne
of the Lord has been removed from this world, and
will "be no more, until he come whose right it is,"
and then it will be given him. And *that time* is the
end of this world, and the beginning of "the world to
come." Therefore while this world stands, a true theocracy can never be in it again. Consequently, from

the death of Christ till the end of this world, every theory of an earthly theocracy is a false theory ; every pretension to it is a false pretension ; and wherever any such theory is proposed or advocated, whether in Rome in the fourth century, or here in the nineteenth century, it bears in it all that the papacy is or that it ever pretended to be, — it puts a man in the place of God.

Now I will read another statement as to the purpose of the Woman's Christian Temperance Union. It is from the annual address of the President of the National Union, at the Nashville convention, 1887. It is as follows : —

"The Woman's Christian Temperance Union, local, State, national, and world-wide, has one vital, organic thought, one all-absorbing purpose, one undying enthusiasm, and that is that Christ shall be *this world's king;* —"

Senator Blair. — "Shall be."

Mr. Jones. — "Shall be this world's king."

Senator Blair. — But you are a clergyman, and you read the Bible to us.

Mr. Jones. — I am going to read a passage presently right on this point.

Senator Blair. — Is it not in the same Bible that the time when Christ is to be the king, is the present ?

Mr. Jones. — I am going to read a passage from the Bible in connection with this subject. Allow me to finish this extract : —

"The Woman's Christian Temperance Union, local, State, national, and world-wide, has one vital, organic thought, one all-absorbing purpose, one undying enthusiasm, and that is that Christ shall be *this world's king ;* — yea, verily, THIS WORLD'S KING in its realm of cause and effect, — king of its courts, its camps, its commerce, — king of its colleges and cloisters, — king of its customs and constitutions. . . . The kingdom of Christ must enter the realm of law through the gate-way of politics."

That emphasizes "*this world's king.*" Jesus Christ himself said, " My kingdom is not of this world." Then assuredly the Woman's Christian Temperance Union stands against the words of Jesus Christ, in saying that he shall be this world's king ; and that that kingdom is to enter the realm of the law through the gate-way of politics. Jesus Christ has his entrance through the gate-way of the gospel, and not through politics.

Nor did this purpose end with the Nashville National Woman's Christian Temperance Union convention. The proposition was repeated by the New York national convention last summer, in the following resolution : —

"*Resolved*, That Christ and his gospel, as universal king and code, should be sovereign in our Government and political affairs."

Well, let us apply the resolution. Suppose the gospel were adopted as the code of this Government. It is the duty of every court to act in accordance with the code. There is a statute in that code which says, —

" If thy brother trespass against thee, rebuke him ; and if he repent, forgive him. And if he trespass against thee seven times in a day, and seven times in a day turn again to thee, saying, I repent ; thou shalt forgive him."

Suppose, then, a man steals a horse. He is arrested, tried, and found guilty. He says, " I repent." " Thou shalt forgive him," says the code, and the Government must conform to the code. He is released, and repeats the act ; is again arrested and found guilty. He says, " I repent." " Thou shalt forgive him," says the code.

And if he repeats the offense seven times in a day, and seven times in a day turns to the court, saying, "I repent," the Government must forgive him, for so says that which the Woman's Christian Temperance Union has resolved should be the governmental code.

Any such system as that would destroy civil government in twenty-four hours. This is not saying anything against the Bible, nor against its principles. It is only illustrating the absurd perversion of its principles by these people who want to establish a system of religious legislation here. God's government is moral, and he has made provision for maintaining his government with the forgiveness of transgression. But he has made no such provision for civil government. No such provision can be made, and civil government be maintained. The Bible reveals God's method of saving those who sin against his moral government ; civil government is man's method of preserving order, and has nothing to do with sin, nor the salvation of sinners. If civil government arrests a thief or a murderer and finds him guilty, the penalty must be executed, though the Lord does forgive him.

The theocratical theory referred to seems to pervade the whole body, for the eighth district of the Woman's Christian Temperance Union, at Augusta, Wis., Oct. 2–4, 1888, representing fifteen counties, passed this resolution : —

" *Whereas*, God would have all men honor the Son, even as they honor the Father ; and, —

" *Whereas*, The civil law which Christ gave from Sinai is the only perfect law, and the only law that will secure the rights of all classes ; therefore, —

" *Resolved*, That civil government should recognize Christ as the moral Governor, and his law as the standard of legislation."

The law which Christ gave from Sinai is not a civil
law ; it is the moral law.   But if that be a civil law, and
this a civil government, what in the world does a civil
government want with a *moral* Governor ?   These
excellent women should be informed that civil government is based upon civil law, and has civil governors
only.   Moral government is founded in moral law, and
has a moral Governor only.   Any governmental theory
that confounds these is a theocratical theory, which is
precisely the governmental theory of the Woman's
Christian Temperance Union, as is demonstrated by
these proofs.   And any theocratical theory of government since Christ died, is the theory of the papacy.

These extracts prove that the purpose of the Woman's
Christian Temperance Union *is* the establishment of " a
practical theocracy."   Please do not misunderstand me
here.   There are none who have more respect or more
good wishes for the Woman's Christian Temperance
Union, in the line of its legitimate work, than have we.
We are heartily in favor of union, of temperance union,
of Christian temperance union, and of woman's Christian temperance union ; but we are *not* in favor of any
kind of political Christian temperance union, nor of
theocratical temperance union.   We sincerely wish
that the Woman's Christian Temperance Union would
stick to its text, and work for Christian temperance
by Christian means ; and not for Christian temperance
by political means, nor for political temperance by
theocratical means.   I believe in Christian temperance.
Not only do I believe in it, but I practice it.   I practice
Christian temperance more strictly than the Woman's
Christian Temperance Union even preaches it.   But
believing in it as thoroughly as I do, and endeavoring
to practice it as strictly as I believe in it, I would never

lift my hand nor open my lips in any effort to *compel* men to practice the Christian temperance in which I believe and which I practice. Christianity persuades men, instead of trying to compel them. By the purity and love of Christ, Christianity draws men instead of trying to drive them. It is not by the power of civil government, but by the power of the Holy Spirit, that Christianity secures the obedience of men and the practice of Christian temperance.

The establishment of a theocracy is the aim of the prime movers in this Sunday-law movement, as it was also the aim of the church leaders of the fourth century. And what came of that movement at that time? I read again : —

"This theocratical theory was already the prevailing one in the time of Constantine ; and . . . the bishops voluntarily made themselves dependent on him by their disputes, *and by their determination to make use of the power of the State for the furtherance of their aims.*" — *Neander, p. 132.*

This being their theory, which resulted in the determination "to make use of the power of the State for the furtherance of their aims," the question arises, What means did they employ to secure control of this power? The answer is, They did it *by means of Sunday laws.*

The first and greatest aim of the political church managers of that time was the exaltation of themselves ; and second only to that was the exaltation of Sunday. These two things had been the principal aim of the bishops of Rome for more than a hundred years, when Constantine gave them a chance to make their schemes effectual by the power of the State. The arrogant pretensions of the bishop of Rome to secure power over the whole church, was first asserted in behalf of Sunday by Victor, who was bishop of Rome from A. D. 193 to 202

"He wrote an imperious letter to the Asiatic prelates commanding them to imitate the example of the Western Christians with respect to the time of celebrating the festival of Easter [that is, commanding them to celebrate it on Sunday]. The Asiatics answered this lordly requisition . . . with great spirit and resolution, that they would by no means depart in this manner from the custom handed down to them by their ancestors. Upon this the thunder of excommunication began to roar. Victor, exasperated by this resolute answer of the Asiatic bishops, broke communion with them, pronounced them unworthy of the name of his brethren, and excluded them from all fellowship with the church of Rome." — *Mosheim, chap. 4, par. 11.*

The one means by which these church managers secured from Constantine the use of the power of the State, was the famous edict prohibiting certain kinds of work on "the venerable day of the sun." That edict runs thus : —

"Let all the judges and towns-people and the occupation of all trades rest on the venerable day of the sun ; but let those who are situated in the country, freely and at full liberty attend to the business of agriculture, because it often happens that no other day is so fit for sowing corn and planting vines, lest the critical moment being let slip, men should lose the commodities granted by Heaven."

This edict was issued March 7, A. D. 321. Only judges and towns-people and mechanics were to rest on Sunday ; people in the country were at full liberty to work. But this did not satisfy the political managers of the churches for any great length of time. "The object of the first Sunday law," says Sozomen. "was that the day might be devoted with less interruption to the purposes of devotion." And as the government was now a theocracy, it was only consistent that all should be required to be religious. Consequently, an additional Sunday law was secured, which commanded *all* people to do no work on Sunday.

"By a law of the year 386, those older changes effected by the Emperor Constantine were more rigorously enforced, and, in general, civil transactions of every kind on Sunday were strictly forbidden. Whoever transgressed was to be considered in fact as guilty of sacrilege." — *Neander, p. 300.*

Then as the people were not allowed to do any manner of work, they would play, and as the natural consequence, the circuses and the theaters throughout the empire were crowded every Sunday. But the object of the law, from the first one that was issued, was that the day might be used for the purposes of devotion, and that the people might go to church. Consequently, that this object might be met, there was another step to take, and it was taken. At a church convention held at Carthage in 401, the bishops passed a resolution to send up a petition to the emperor, praying —

"That the public shows might be transferred from the Christian Sunday, and from feast-days, to some other days of the week." — *Idem.*

History does not say whether or not this petition represented the names of fourteen million petitioners, the greater part of whom never signed it at all. History is also silent as to whether the petition was indorsed by any one man who could be counted for seven million two hundred thousand men. But history is *not* silent as to the reason why it was necessary to send up the petition. The petitioners themselves gave the reason, and it was this ; —

"The people congregate more to the circus than to the church."—*Idem, note 5.*

In the circuses and the theaters large numbers of men were employed, among whom many were church-members. But rather than to give up their jobs, they would work on Sunday. The bishops complained that these were compelled to work: they pronounced it persecution, and asked for a law to protect those persons from such "persecution." The church had become filled with a mass of people, unconverted, who cared vastly more for worldly interests and pleasures than they did for religion. And as the government was now a government of God, it was considered proper that the civil power should be used to cause all to show respect for God, whether or not they belonged to a church, or whether they had any respect for God.

The people, not being allowed to work, crowded the circus and the theater. They had no wish to be devoted; and as they were forced to be idle, a flood of dissipation was the inevitable consequence. Neander says of it:—

"Owing to the prevailing passion at that time, especially in the large cities, to run after the various public shows, it so happened that when these spectacles fell on the same days which had been consecrated by the church to some religious festival, they proved a great hinderance to the devotion of Christians, though chiefly, it must be allowed, to those whose Christianity was the least an affair of the life and of the heart." — *Idem.*

And further:—

"Church teachers . . . were in truth often forced to complain that in such competitions the theater was vastly more frequented than the church." — *Idem.*

And the church could not then stand competition; she wanted a monopoly. She got it, at last.

This petition of the Carthage Convention could not
be granted at once, but in the year 425, the desired law
was secured ; and to this also there was attached the
reason that was given for the first Sunday law that ever
was made ; namely, —

"In order that the devotion of the faithful might be
free from all disturbance." — *Idem, p. 301.*

It must constantly be borne in mind, however, that
the only way in which "the devotion of the faithful"
was "disturbed" by these things, was that when the
circus or the theater was open at the same time that
the church was open, the "faithful" would go to the
circus or the theater instead of to church, and *therefore*
their "devotion" was "disturbed." And of course the
only way in which the "devotion" of such "faithful"
ones could be freed from all disturbance, was to close
the circuses and the theaters at church time. Thus,
and by this means, every reason for not being devoted
was taken away from all the people. Then in the very
next sentence Neander says : —

"In this way the church received help from the State
for the furtherance of her ends."

This statement is correct. Constantine did many
things to favor the bishops. He gave them money and
political preference. He made their decisions in dis-
puted cases as final as the decision of Jesus Christ. But
in nothing that he did for them did he give them power
over those who did not belong to the church, to compel
them to act as though they did, except in that one thing
of the Sunday law. Their decisions, which he decreed
to be final, were binding only on those who voluntarily
chose that tribunal, and affected none others. Before
this time, if any who had repaired to the tribunal of the

bishops were dissatisfied with the decision, they could appeal to the civil magistrate. This edict cut off that source of appeal, yet affected none but those who voluntarily chose the arbitration of the bishops. But in the Sunday law, power was given to the church to compel those who did not belong to the church, and who were not subject to the jurisdiction of the church, to obey the commands of the church. In the Sunday law there was given to the church control of the civil power, that by it she could compel those who did not belong to the church to act as if they did. The history of Constantine's time may be searched through and through, and it will be found that in nothing did he give to the church any such power, except in this one thing — the Sunday law. Neander's statement is literally correct, that it was " in this way the church received help from the State for the furtherance of her ends."

The work, however, was not done yet. True, the bishops had secured the power of the State to take away from the people all excuse for not being religious ; but from the beginning of the whole scheme, the people had no real wish to be religious. They had none of the spirit of devotion in their hearts ; and although the State had forbidden them to work, and had shut the Sunday circuses and theaters, still the people would not be religious. The next step to be taken, therefore, in the logic of the situation, was to *compel* them ; and the theocratical bishops were equal to the occasion. They were ready with a theory that exactly met the demands of the case ; and the great Catholic Church Father and Catholic saint, Augustine, was the father of this Catholic saintly theory. He wrote : —

" It is indeed better that men should be brought to serve God by instruction than by fear of punishment, or

THE FOUNDATION OF THE INQUISITION.

by pain. But because the former means are better, the latter must not therefore be neglected. . . . Many must often be brought back to their Lord, like wicked servants, by the rod of temporal suffering, before they attain to the highest grade of religious development."—*Schaff's Church History, vol. 2, sec. 27.*

Of this theory Neander remarks : —

"It was by Augustine, then, that a theory was proposed and founded, which . . . contained the germ of that whole system of spiritual despotism, of intolerance and persecution, which ended in the tribunals of the Inquisition." — *Church History, p. 217.*

The history of the Inquisition is only the history of the carrying out of this infamous theory of Augustine's. But this theory is only the logical sequence of the theory upon which the whole series of Sunday laws was founded. The church induced the State to compel all to be idle for their own good. Then it was found that they all were more inclined to wickedness. Then to save them from all going to the Devil, they tried to compel all to go to heaven. The work of the Inquisition was always for love of men's souls, and to save them from hell !

Allow me to summarize these statements from Neander : He says of the carrying into effect of the theocratical theory of those bishops, that they made themselves dependent upon Constantine by their disputes, and "by their determination to use the power of the State for the furtherance of their aims." Then he mentions the first and second Sunday laws of Constantine ; the Sunday law of 386 ; the Carthage Convention, resolution, and petition of 401 ; and the law of 425 in response to this petition ; and then, without a break, and with direct reference to these Sunday laws, he says: "*In this way* the church received help from the State for the furtherance of her ends." She started out with the determination to do it ; she did it ; and "*in this way*" she did it. And when she had secured the control of the power of the State, she used it for the furtherance of her own aims, and in her own despotic way, as announced in Augustine's Inquisitorial theory. The first step logically and inevitably led to the last ; and the theocratical leaders in the movement had the cruel courage to follow the first step unto the last, as framed in the words of Augustine, and illustrated in the history of the Inquisition.

That is the system with which Sunday laws belong. That is the theory upon which they are based. They have no other foundation. Mr. Elliott, who has spoken here in behalf of this bill, knows that there is no law in the Bible for keeping the first day of the week. I could read a passage from his own book, " The Abiding Sabbath," page 184, in which he confesses "the complete silence of the New Testament, so far as any explicit command for the Sabbath, or definite rules for its observance, are concerned." And everybody knows that the Old Testament does not say anything about the observance of the first day of the week as Sabbath. Everybody likewise knows that the Old Testament does not say anything about keeping the first day of the week as the day of the resurrection of the Saviour, or for any other reason. Dr. Johnson and others here this morning have said that the first day of the week was chosen because it was a memorial of the resurrection of the Saviour. It is the New Testament that tells about the resurrection of the Saviour. That is granted. Dr. Elliott confesses, and the American Tract Society publishes it, that there is "complete silence of the New Testament" in regard to it. Then what right have they to put it into a law, and try to compel by civil law all people to keep as the Lord's day that for which there is no scriptural authority?   Let me read another passage from another book, printed by the American Sunday-school Union.   On page 186 of "The Lord's Day," written by Mr. A. E. Waffle, are these words : —

"Up to the time of Christ's death, no change had been made in the day.   The authority must be sought in the words or in the example of the inspired apostles."

Then on the very next page he says : —

"So far as the record shows, they [the apostles] did not, however, give any explicit command enjoining the abandonment of the seventh-day Sabbath, and its observance on the first day of the week."

Dr. Schaff, in the Schaff Herzog Cyclopedia, says : —

"No regulations for its observance are laid down in the New Testament, nor, indeed, is its observance even enjoined." — *Article Sunday.*

If, then, they confess that Christ gave no law for its observance, why do they want to compel people to observe it?   What right have they to compel anybody to observe it?   I deny their right to compel me or anybody else to do what Christ never commanded any man to do.

Senator Blair. — You admit there was a Sabbath before Christ came?

Mr. Jones. — Certainly.

Senator Blair. — And he said he came not to destroy, but to fulfill?

Mr. Jones. — Certainly.

Senator Blair. — Is there anything in the New Testament which destroyed the Sabbath already existing?

Mr. Jones. — No, sir.

Senator Blair. — Then why does it not continue to exist?

Mr. Jones. — It does exist, and we keep the commandment which provides for the Sabbath.

Senator Blair. — Then you say there is a Sabbath recognized, and that is equivalent to its re-affirmation by Christ?

Mr. Jones. — Certainly.

Senator Blair. — I do not see from what you are stating, but that Christ recognized an existing law, and that it is continuing at the present time. You say that it is one day, and they say that it is another.

Mr. Jones. — But they are after a law to enforce the observance of the first day of the week as the Lord's day, when they confess that the Lord never gave any command in regard to it. The commandment which God gave says that the "seventh day is the Sabbath."

Senator Blair. — Is it still the Sabbath?

Mr. Jones. — Certainly, and we keep it; but we deny the right of any civil government to compel any man either to keep it or not to keep it.

Senator Blair. — The civil government of the Jews compelled its observance?

Mr. Jones. — That was a theocracy.

Senator Blair. — Does it follow that when the only form of government is a theocracy and that embraces all that appertains to government, another form of government which is not a theocracy necessarily, cannot embrace the same subject-matter as the theocracy? If the subject-matter of a theocratical, a monarchial, or a republican form of government is not the same, to control the establishment of good order in society, pray what is it? We say, and it is our form of government, that the people shall legislate, shall construe the law, and execute the law. Under the old theocratic form, God made the law, God construed it, and God executed it through his instrumentalities; but we do just the same thing by the will of the people, that under the theocratic form of government was done in the other way. Now if the Sabbath is necessarily for the general good of society, a republican form of government must make and enforce the observance of the Sabbath just as the theocracy did. You seem to be laboring, as it strikes me, under the impression that a civil government for the good of the people carried on by us under the republican form, cannot do anything that the theocratic form of government does when the theocratic is the only form. They necessarily cover the same subject-matter, — the control, the development, the good, and the health of society, it makes no difference which one it may be.

Mr. Jones. — A theocratic government is a government of God.

Senator Blair. — So are the powers that be ordained of God.

Mr. Jones. — This Government is not a government of God.

Senator Blair. — Do you not consider the Government of the United States as existing in accordance with the will of God ?

Mr. Jones. — Yes, but it is not a government of God. The government of God is a moral government. This is a *civil* government.

Senator Blair. — A theocracy is a civil government, and governs in civil affairs, as well as in the region of spirituality and morality and religion.

Mr. Jones. — Certainly, and God governs it, and nothing but a theocracy can enforce those things which pertain to man's relation to God under the first four commandments.

Senator Blair. — But this proposed legislation is outside of the theocratic part of it.

Mr. Jones. — Not at all ; for it proposes by penalties to " promote" the religious observance of the Lord's day, while nothing but the government of God can do that.   That is the point I am making here, that if you allow this legislation, you lead to the establishment of a new theocracy after the model of the papacy, and civil government has nothing to do with religious things. This bill is wholly religious ; and if you begin this course of religious legislation, you will end only in a theocracy, — a man-made theocracy, — and that will be the papacy repeated.

Senator Blair. — We have had the Sunday laws in this country for three hundred years.   They have constantly become more and more liberalized.   Have you ever known an instance, though the sentiment in favor of the Sabbath seems to be growing constantly stronger, where any State in this Union undertook to enact a law that anybody should go to church, which is the danger you seem to apprehend ?

Mr. Jones. — Not yet.   They are now after the first law.   This will lead to that.   The law of Constantine was enacted in 321, and it commanded at first only that towns-people and mechanics should do no work, that they might be religious.   They did not ask for too much at first.   As was said in a ministers' meeting in San Diego, Cal., about two months ago, " In this thing you must not ask for too much at first.   Ask just what public sentiment will bear, and when you get that, ask for more."   And as was said upon this bill by Dr. Crafts in this Capitol, —

"*We will take a quarter of a loaf, half a loaf, or a whole loaf.* If the Government should do nothing more than forbid the opening of the post-offices at church hours, it would be a national tribute to the value of religion, and would lead to something more satisfactory."

Then in telling what would be more satisfactory, he said : —

"The law allows the local postmaster, if he chooses (and some of them do choose), to open the mails at the very hour of church, and so make the post-office the competitor of the churches."

At another point in the same speech, Mr. Crafts referred to the proposed law as one for "protecting the church services from post-office competition." And in explaining how this could be done, he said : —

"A law forbidding the opening between ten and twelve, would accomplish this, and would be better than nothing ; *but we want more.*"

And, —

"A law forbidding any handling of Sunday mail at such hours as would interfere with church attendance on the part of the employees, would be better than nothing ; *but we want more than this.*"

He continues : —

"Local option in deciding whether a local post-office shall be opened at all on Sunday, we should welcome as better than nothing ; . . . *but we desire more than this.*"

How much more ? Still he continues : —

"A law forbidding all carrier delivery of mail on Sunday, would be better than nothing ; *but we want more than that.*"

And when will they ever get enough ? It is precisely as it was when the Emperor Constantine forbade the judges, towns-people, and mechanics to work on Sunday. That was an imperial tribute to the "value of religion," and led to "something more satisfactory"—to the church managers.

Senator Blair.—Have you ever heard of a proposition's being made in any legislative body to compel any one to attend church on Sunday?

Mr. Jones.—The propositions that are made are for that very purpose, to stop the Sunday trains, the Sunday newspapers,—in short, to stop all work on Sunday, *so that the people can go to church.*

Senator Blair.—But these people come here and say that they have no such purpose, and they have been doing these things in the States for a hundred years, and during the Colonial period anterior to that time. Have you ever heard on the American continent, within the territory of what is now the United States, a proposition or a suggestion in a legislative body to compel anybody to attend church?

Mr. Jones.—Not in a legislative body, but in ecclesiastical bodies.

Senator Blair.—Ecclesiastical bodies do not make the laws. Congress is not an ecclesiastical body.

Mr. Jones.—But it is an ecclesiastical body that is seeking to secure and enforce this law, just as the New England theocracy did when "absence from 'the ministry of the word' was punished by a fine;" and then when people were compelled under such penalty to go to church and listen to the preaching, it was such preaching as, said one of the victims, "was meat to be digested, but only by the heart or stomacke of an ostrich."

Nor was this confined to Colonial times or to New England; for after the Colonies became States, North

Carolina had a Sunday law, — has yet, for aught I know, — reading as follows : —

"Be it enacted . . . that all and every person or persons shall on the Lord's day, commonly called Sunday, carefully apply themselves to the duties of religion and piety."

In 1803, Tennessee passed a law embodying the same words. But South Carolina and Georgia went farther than this ; South Carolina enacted that —

"All and every person whatsoever, shall, on every Lord's day, apply themselves to the observation of the same, by exercising themselves thereon in the duties of piety and true religion, publicly and privately ; and having no reasonable or lawful excuse, on every Lord's day shall resort to their parish church, or some other parish church, or some meeting or assembly of religious worship."

In 1803, Georgia likewise enacted a Sunday law whose first section required all persons to attend public worship. In 1821, the State of Connecticut, in revising its laws, made its Sunday law read in the first section, that —

"It shall be the duty of the citizens of this State to attend the public worship of God on the Lord's day."

This is precisely the line of things proposed by these men and women now working for this Sunday law. This is the first step in that direction. The whole object which they have in view in stopping work on Sunday, is identical with that of the fourth century ; namely, in order that the people may be devoted, in order that they may go to church. The very intention of these men in securing the law is religious.

I will refer you to some of the statements of the very men who stood in this room this forenoon, arguing

6

for this Sunday bill.   Dr. W. W. Everts, of Chicago, in a Sunday-law convention in Illinois, Nov. 8, 1887, declared Sunday to be the "test of all religion."   Taking his own words, what can the enforcement of it ever be but the enforcement of a religious test?   Dr. Crafts, who is so prominent in this work, said to the Knights of Labor at Indianapolis, as I have before quoted, and he repeated it in this city last night, "If you take *religion* out of the day, you take the *rest* out of it."   This statement was made in reply to a question as to whether a day of rest could not be secured to the working-men without reference to religion.   Taking the statement of Dr. Crafts, therefore, its being a day of rest to anybody depends altogether upon whether religion is in it; for if you take religion out, you take the rest out.   He, with these others, demands a law compelling the people to take the *rest*.   Religion being in the rest, and the rest wholly dependent upon the fact that religion is in it, it is inevitable that their effort to secure a law compelling everybody to rest on Sunday is an effort to establish by law a religious observance.

Again : in the Boston Monday lectureship of 1887, Joseph Cook said, —

"The experience of centuries shows that you will in vain endeavor to preserve Sunday as a day of rest, unless you preserve it *as a day of worship*."

Further : Dr. Everts said in the Elgin convention :—

"The laboring class are apt to rise late on Sunday morning, read the Sunday papers, and allow the *hour of worship* to go by unheeded."

And in Chicago only three weeks ago, Dr. Herrick Johnson named the matter with which he said the Sunday papers are filled — crime, scandal, gossip, news, and politics — and exclaimed : —

"What a *melange!* what a dish to set down before a man before breakfast and after breakfast, *to prepare him for hearing the word of God!* It makes it twice as hard to reach those who go to the sanctuary, and it *keeps many away from the house of worship altogether."*

Dr. Everts said further in the Elgin convention : —

"The Sunday train is another great evil. They cannot afford to run a train unless they get a great many passengers, and *so break up a great many congregations.* The Sunday railroad trains are hurrying their passengers fast on to perdition. What an outrage that the railroad, that great civilizer, should destroy the Christian Sabbath!"

I will give one more statement which sums up the whole matter. In a Sunday-law mass-meeting held in Hamilton Hall, Oakland, Cal., in January, 1887, Rev. Dr. Briggs, of Napa, Cal., said to the State : —

"You relegate moral instruction to the church, and then let all go as they please on Sunday, so that we cannot get at them."

Therefore they want the State to *corral* all the people on Sunday, so that the preachers can get at them.

These statements might be multiplied indefinitely ; but these are enough. The speeches, and the sermons, and the work, of those who are in favor of the Sunday laws, are all in the same line. They all plainly show that the secret and real object of the whole Sunday-law movement is to get the people to go to church. The Sunday train must be stopped, because church members ride on it, and do n't go to church enough. The Sunday paper must be abolished, because the people read it instead of going to church, and because those who read it and go to church too, are not so well prepared to receive the preaching.

It was precisely the same way in the fourth century concerning the Sunday circus and theater. The people, even the church members, would go to these instead of to church ; and even if they went to both, it must be confessed that the Roman circus or theater was not a very excellent dish — " What a *melange!* " — to set down before a man to prepare him for hearing the word of God. The Sunday circus and theater could not afford to keep open unless they could get a great many spectators, and so break up a great many congregations ; and as they hurried the spectators fast on to perdition, they had to be shut on Sunday, so as to keep " a great many congregations " out of perdition. It is exceedingly difficult to see how a Sunday circus in the fourth century could hurry to perdition any one who did not attend it ; or how a Sunday train in the nineteenth century can hurry to perdition any one who does not ride on it. And if any are hurried to perdition by this means, who is to blame : the Sunday train, or the ones who ride on it ? And Dr. Johnson's complaint of the Sunday papers, is of the same flimsy piece. If the Sunday paper gets into a man's house, where lies the blame : upon the paper, or upon the one who takes it and reads it ? Right here lies the secret of the whole evil now, as it did in the fourth century : they blame everybody and everything else, even to inanimate things, for the irreligion, the infidelity, and the sin that lie in their own hearts.

When they shall have stopped all Sunday work, and all Sunday papers, and all Sunday trains, in order that the people may go to church and attend to things divine, suppose that then the people fail to go to church or attend to things divine : will the religio-political managers stop there ? Having done all this that the people may be devoted, will they suffer their good intentions to be frustrated, or their good offices to be despised? Will not these now take the next logical step, — the step that was taken in the fourth century, — and *compel* men to attend to things divine? Having taken all the steps but this, will they not take this? Having compelled men to rest, will they stop short of an effort to supply the religious sanctions which alone can prevent a day of enforced rest from being a day of enforced idleness, and consequently of wickedness? The probability that they will not is strengthened by the fact that the theory upon which this is carried on is identical with that of the fourth century — the theory of a theocracy.

I have cited the theocratical purpose of the Woman's Christian Temperance Union. The National Reform Association, whose secretary stood at this table to-day to plead for the passage of this bill, aims directly at the establishment of a theocracy in this Government. In their own words, they propose to make this republic "as truly and really a theocracy as the commonwealth of Israel."

The Sunday-law Association also holds much the same theory. In the Elgin Sunday-law convention, Dr. Mandeville, of Chicago, said : —

" The merchants of Tyre insisted upon selling goods near the temple on the Sabbath, and Nehemiah compelled the officers of the law to do their duty, and stop it. So we can compel the officers of the law to do their duty."

Nehemiah was ruling there in a true theocracy, a government of God ; the law of God was the law of the land, and God's will was made known by the written word, and by the prophets. Therefore if Dr. Mandeville's argument is of any force at all, it is so only upon

the claim of the establishment of a theocracy. With
this idea the view of Dr. Crafts agrees precisely, and
Dr. Crafts is general field secretary for the National
Sunday-law Union. He claims, as expressed in his
own words, that —

"The preachers are the successors of the prophets."
— *Christian Statesman, July 5, 1888.*

Now put these things together. The government of
Israel was.a theocracy; the will of God was made
known to the ruler by prophets; the ruler compelled
the officers of the law to prevent the ungodly from
selling goods on the Sabbath. This government is to
be made a theocracy; the preachers are the successors
of the prophets; and they are to compel the officers of
the law to prevent all selling of goods and all manner
of work on Sunday. This shows conclusively that these
preachers intend to take the supremacy into their hands,
officially declare the will of God, and compel all men to
conform to it. And this deduction is made certain by
the words of Prof. Blanchard, in the Elgin convention : —

"In this work we are undertaking for the Sabbath,
we are the representatives of God."

And the chief of these representatives of God, will
be but a pope again ; because when preachers control
the civil power as the representatives of God, a pope is
inevitable.

These quotations prove, to a demonstration, that the
whole theory upon which this religio-political movement is based, is identical with that of the fourth century, which established the papacy. They show also
that the means employed — Sunday laws — by which
to gain control of the civil power to make the wicked

tneory effective, are identical with the means which were employed in the fourth century for the same purpose. The next question is, Will they carry the theory into effect as they did in the fourth century and onward? In other words, when they get the power to oppress, will they use the power? A sufficient answer to this would seem to be the simple inquiry, If they do not intend to use the power, then why are they making such strenuous efforts to get it? If Congress lets them have the power, they will surely use it. Human nature is the same now as it was in the fourth century. Politics is the same now as it was then. And as for religious bigotry, it knows no centuries; it knows no such thing as progress or enlightenment; it is ever the same. And in its control of civil power, the cruel results are also ever the same

How appropriate, therefore, is it that Cardinal Gibbons should indorse the national Sunday bill! How natural, indeed, that he should gladly add his name to the number of petitioners in support of the movement to secure legislation in the interests of the church! He knows just how his brethren in the fourth century worked the same kind of scheme; he knows what the outcome of the movement was then; and he knows full well what the outcome of this movement will be now. He knows that the theory underlying this movement is identical with the theory which was the basis of that; he knows the methods of working are the same now as they were then; he knows that the means employed to secure control of the civil power now, are identical with the means employed then; and he knows that the result must be the same. He knows that when religion shall have been established as an essential element in legislation in this Government, the experience of fifteen hundred eventful years, and "the ingenuity and patient care" of fifty generations of statesmen, will not be lost in the effort to make the papal power supreme over all here and now, as was done there and then. And in carrying out the instructions of Pope Leo XIII., that "all Catholics should do all in their power to cause the constitutions of States and legislation to be modeled upon the principles of the true church," the Cardinal assuredly *is* glad to have the opportunity to add his name to the more than six millions of Protestants who are set for the accomplishment of the same task.

To those Protestants who are so anxious to make religion a subject of legislation, it now appears very desirable ; and it also appears a very pleasant thing to secure the alliance of the papacy. But when they shall have accomplished the feat, and find themselves in the midst of a continuous whirl of political strife and contention with the papacy, not alone for supremacy, but for *existence*, — then they will find it not nearly so desirable as it now appears to their vision, blinded by the lust for illegitimate power.

And when they find themselves compelled to pay more than they bargained to, they will have but themselves to blame ; for when they make religion a subject of legislation, they therein confess that it is justly subject to the rule of majorities. And then, if the Romish Church secures the majority, and compels the Protestants to conform to Catholic forms and ordinances, the Protestants cannot justly complain. Knowing, as we do, the outcome of the same kind of movement before, we do not propose to allow this scheme to be worked out here without a decided protest.

Senator Blair. — You are entirely logical, because you say there should be no Sunday legislation by State or nation either.

Mr. Jones. — Yes, sir, of course I am logical, all the way through. I want to show you the wicked principle upon which this whole system is founded, and the reason I do this is because the last step is involved in the first one. If you allow this principle and this movement to take the first step, those who get the power will see in the end that they take the last step. That is the danger. See how in the fourth century the logic of it ended only with the Inquisition.

Senator Blair. — Was the Inquisition abolished by the abolition of the Sunday laws?

Mr. Jones. — No ; but the principle of it was established by Sunday laws.

Senator Blair. — Then if the Inquisition was established by the Sunday laws, how was it abolished, but by the abolition of the Sabbath? How can you remove an effect except by removing its cause?

Mr. Jones. — The Sunday laws never have been abolished.

Senator Blair. — Then the Sunday law could not have been the cause of the Inquisition.

Mr. Jones. — The power which embodies the Inquisition still continues, and its emissaries have been in this country defending the Inquisition. That same power is now grasping for the control of the civil law, and the same causes generally produce the same effects.

Senator Blair. — And the removal of the causes removes the effects with them.

Mr. Jones. — Sometimes.

Senator Blair. — Therefore the Sunday laws were not the cause of the Inquisition, unless the Inquisition still exists.

Mr. Jones. — No, the Sunday laws did not *cause* the Inquisition.

Senator Blair. — I understood you to say that it did.

Mr. Jones. — I say, through that the church received the power to make the principle and the work of the Inquisition effective. A certain exercise of power may be forbidden, and yet the means by which the power was obtained may not be forbidden. In other words, the power which was obtained through the deception of Sunday laws, may be prohibited in certain things, and yet allowed in many other things.

Senator Blair. — The Lord made the Sabbath, and governed the Jewish nation for nearly three thousand years with a Sabbath. Do you think the Sabbath was for the good of the Jewish people, or for their injury?

Mr. Jones. — It was established for the good of the human race.

Senator Blair. — Including the Jewish people?

Mr. Jones. — Yes, sir.

Senator Blair. — It was established as a part of the civil administration.

Mr. Jones. — But the church and the State were one.

Senator Blair. — Therefore what we call the civil administration was included in that theocracy.

Mr. Jones. — The church and the State were one. They were united, and it was a theocracy.

Senator Blair. — If the administration of the Sabbath during these three thousand years, at least, was for the good of the Jews and the human race, why will not the Sabbath be good for the Jews and the human race since the time of Christ, as well as before?

Mr. Jones. — It is for the good of the human race.

Senator Blair. — The civil law must administrate it if it is done. Then we will get no Sabbath now under our division of powers of government, unless we have the Sabbath recognized and enforced by the State authority?

Mr. Jones. — Certainly we have a Sabbath.

Senator Blair. — Your proposition is to strike out the Sabbath from the Constitution and condition of society in these modern times?

Mr. Jones. — No, sir.

Senator Blair. — Certainly so far as its existence and enactment and enforcement by law are concerned.

Mr. Jones. — Yes, by civil law.

Senator Blair. — It was enforced in what we call the civil conduct of men under that theocratic form of government for at least three thousand years.

Mr. Jones. — Certainly.

Senator Blair. — Now the observance of the Sabbath depends upon a compulsory observance of the law.

Mr. Jones. — Not at all.

Senator Blair. — It required the law of God which he enforced by death, by stoning men to death when they violated it, and we have the Sabbath day only by virtue of what we call the civil law, which is equally a part of God's law.

Mr. Jones. — That government was not organized specially to enforce the Sabbath.

Senator Blair. — They stoned men to death who violated the law.

Mr. Jones. — Certainly; and likewise for the transgression of the other commandments.

Senator Blair. — God enforced it, in other words, by human means.

Mr. Jones. — Certainly; my answer to all that is that that was a theocracy, — a union of church and state. The church was the State, and the State was the church.

Senator Blair. — You say now that there is no State to enforce it?

Mr. Jones. — I say that no government can enforce the Sabbath, or those things which pertain to God, except a theocratic government — a union of church and state. Therefore I say that if you establish such a law as is here proposed, you lead directly to a union of church and state. The logic of the question demands it, and that is where it will end, because the law cannot be enforced otherwise. These gentlemen say they do not want a union of church and state. What they mean by church and state is, for the State to select one particular denomination, and make it the favorite above all other denominations. That is a union of church and state according to their idea. But a union of church and state was formed by Constantine when he recognized Christianity as the religion of the Roman empire. Everybody knows that that was a union of church and state, and that it ended in the papacy. A union of church and state is where the ecclesiastical power controls the civil power, and uses the civil power in its own interests. That is where this movement will end, and that is one of the reasons why we oppose it.

Senator Blair. — You say the church and state separated shall not do those proper things which the church and state always did when united in the theocracy?

Mr. Jones. — No, sir.

Senator Blair. — Then why do you say that the state —

Mr. Jones. — I did not mean to deny your proposition; I think the way you intended, I mean "Yes," because I certainly do say that the church and state separated shall do those proper things which were done when they were united in the theocracy.

Senator Blair. — If in this division of the powers of

government into church and state, you exclude from the powers of the church the establishment and enforcement and regulation of the Sabbath, why do you not necessarily, if the Sabbath is a good thing, pass it over to the control of the State?

Mr. Jones. — Because if the church will not recognize it and preserve it, the State cannot compel people to do it. The State that attempts it is bound to fail.

Senator Blair. — Then you necessarily take the ground that God did wrong in the enforcement of the Sabbath during those three thousand years when his government was both church and state.

Mr. Jones. — No, sir. If God would come himself to govern, and make himself governor, as he did of Israel, he could enforce the law as he did there. But until God does that, we deny the right of all the churches or anybody else, to do it.

Senator Blair. — Even if it is for the good of society?

Mr. Jones. — What they say is for the good of society is for the ruin of society.

Senator Blair. — Do you understand that it is the church or the State that is making this law?

Mr. Jones. — It is the State that is doing it, just as Constantine did it, *to satisfy the churches.*

Senator Blair. — It may or may not satisfy the churches. The churches give their reasons here, which may be right or wrong, for the establishment of the Sabbath — for this Sunday legislation in all the States. The State, the whole people, make the law. You say that the whole people shall not make a good law because the churches ask for it.

Mr. Jones. — I say the whole people shall not make a bad law, even though the churches do demand it; for any civil law relating to God is a bad law.

Senator Blair. — Then what God did for three thousand years for the good of the Jews and the human race, was wrong?

Mr. Jones. — No, sir; it was right.

Senator Blair. — Then why not continue it?

Mr. Jones. — Because he has discontinued that kind of government.

Senator Blair. — We have done nothing in the world to divide the powers of government into those of church and state. We say those departments shall not interfere with each other.

Mr. Jones. — Certainly.

Senator Blair. — Here and in the States we are trying to run the civil parts. We have taken jurisdiction of a portion of what God has entire jurisdiction, as to the church and state in the civil relations of men. The entire society does that. We put the sovereignty into the hands of everybody except women, and some of us are trying to do that. We have the same subject-matter, the good of society under our control, which under the theocracy was united into both church and state. If you do not let the State continue to do what was essential to society then, and is now, you are striking at one of the great ends for which government exists.

Mr. Jones. — Not at all; because God has discontinued that kind of government.

Senator Blair. — He has not discontinued the necessity of laws for the regulation of society.

Mr. Jones. — He has in that way.

Senator Blair. — No; it is just as necessary that there should be a Sabbath now for the good of man, as when God made and enforced the law by his direct supervision under a theocracy.

Mr. Jones. — But no government but a theocracy can enforce such laws.

Senator Blair. — Then unless we have a theocracy, we shall have no Sabbath.

Mr. Jones. — We shall have no laws regulating the Sabbath.

Senator Blair. — The Sabbath did not descend to the Jews and to all mankind, because there was a theo-cratic form of government among the Jews. How did the Sabbath come to mankind at large, when there was no theocratic form of government?

Mr. Jones. — Those nations never kept it. Nobody but the Jews ever kept it.

Senator Blair. — They could have kept it, because you say the Sabbath existed for all; not for the Jews alone, but for the human race.

Mr. Jones. — Certainly, but if they did not keep it, it would do no good.

Senator Blair. — It did not exist for good, then?

Mr. Jones. — Certainly; a thing may exist for my good, and I may refuse to use it, as thousands do the salvation of Christ.

Senator Blair. — I was taking your statement as true that it did exist for good outside of the Jews.

Mr. Jones. — I said it was for the good of man. The Saviour said it was for the good of man. The Saviour died for the good of man.

Senator Blair. — You would abolish the Sabbath, anyway?

Mr. Jones. — Yes, in the civil law.

Senator Blair. — You would abolish any Sabbath from human practice which shall be in the form of law, unless the individual here and there sees fit to observe it?

Mr. Jones. — Certainly ; that is a matter between man and his God.

Senator Blair. — Your time has expired. Please take five minutes to close, as I have asked you some questions ; still, they were questions that touched the trouble in my own mind.

Mr. Jones. — Certainly ; but I supposed that I was to have an hour to devote, uninterruptedly, to the points in question.

Senator Blair. — We have always been accustomed to conducting these hearings with reference to getting at the difficulties we had in our own minds, and I do not feel as though you could complain with an hour and ten minutes, if we give you ten minutes more.

Mr. Jones. — Very good.   Mr. Chairman, I have shown that in the fourth century this same movement developed a theocracy and in that the papacy, religious despotism, and oppression for conscience' sake.   Now I want to show the secret of at least a portion of the present movement.   The representative of the National Reform Association spoke here in behalf of this proposed legislation.   That Association is asking for such a law and for such an amendment to the Constitution as you have proposed, in relation to the Christian religion in the public schools.   That measure pleases them well, and this proposed Sunday law pleases them well.

Senator Blair. — Just incorporate that. proposed amendment to the Constitution in your remarks.

Mr. Jones. — Very well ; it is as follows : —

"50th CONGRESS, }
    1st SESSION. } S. R. 86.

"Joint Resolution, proposing an amendment to the Constitution of the United States respecting establishments of religion and free public schools.

"*Resolved by the Senate and House of Representatives of the United States of America in Congress assembled (two-thirds of each House concurring therein)*, That the following amendment to the Constitution of the United States be, and hereby is, proposed to the States, to become valid when ratified by the legislatures of three-fourths of the States, as provided in the Constitution : —

"ARTICLE.

"SECTION 1. No State shall ever make or maintain any law respecting an establishment of religion, or prohibiting the free exercise thereof.

"SEC. 2. Each State in this Union shall establish and maintain a system of free public schools adequate for the education of all the children living therein, between the ages of six and sixteen years, inclusive, in the common branches of knowledge, and in virtue, morality, and the principles of the Christian religion. But no money raised by taxation imposed by law, or any money or other property or credit belonging to any municipal organization, or to any State, or to the United States, shall ever be appropriated, applied, or given to the use or purposes of any school, institution, corporation, or person, whereby instruction or training shall be given in the doctrines, tenets, belief, ceremonials, or observances peculiar to any sect, denomination, organization, or society, being, or claiming to be, religious in its character ; nor shall such peculiar doctrines, tenets, belief, ceremonials, or observances be taught or inculcated in the free public schools.

"SEC. 3. To the end that each State, the United States, and all the people thereof, may have and preserve governments republican in form and in substance, the United States shall guaranty to every State, and to the people of every State and of the United States, the support and maintenance of such a system of free public schools as is herein provided.

"SEC. 4. That Congress shall enforce this article by legislation when necessary."

What, then, do these men propose to do with the civil power when they can use it? The *Christian Statesman* is the organ of that Association, and in its issue of Oct. 2, 1884, said : —

" Give all men to understand that this is a Christian nation, and that, believing that without Christianity we perish, we must maintain by all means our Christian character.   Inscribe this character on our Constitution. Enforce upon all who come among us the laws of Christian morality."

To enforce upon men the laws of Christian morality, is nothing else than an attempt to compel them to be Christians, and does in fact compel them to be hypocrites.   It will be seen at once that this will be but to invade the rights of conscience, and this, one of the vice-presidents of the Association declares, civil power has the right to do.   Rev. David Gregg, D. D., now pastor of Park Street Church, Boston, a vice-president of the National Reform Association, plainly declared in the *Christian Statesman* of June 5, 1884, that the civil power " has the right to command the consciences of men."

Rev. M. A. Gault, a district secretary and a leading worker of the Association, says : —

" Our remedy for all these malefic influences, is to have the Government simply set up the moral law and recognize God's authority behind it, and lay its hand on any religion that does not conform to it."

When they have the Government lay its hand on dissenters, what will they have it do ?   Rev. E. B. Graham, also a vice-president of the Association, in an address delivered at York, Neb., and reported in the *Christian Statesman* of May 21, 1885, said : —

" We might add in all justice, If the opponents of the Bible do not like our Government and its Christian features, let them go to some wild, desolate land, and in the name of the Devil, and for the sake of the Devil, subdue it, and set up a government of their own on infidel and atheistic ideas ; and then if they can stand it, stay there till they die."

That is what they propose to do. And that is worse than Russia. In the *Century* for April, 1888, Mr. Kennan gave a view of the statutes of Russia on the subject of crimes against the faith, quoting statute after statute providing that whoever shall censure the Christian faith or the orthodox church, or the Scriptures, or the holy sacraments, or the saints, or their images, or the Virgin Mary, or the angels, or Christ, or God, shall be deprived of all civil rights, and exiled for life to the most remote parts of Siberia. This is the system in Russia, and it is in the direct line of the wishes of the National Reform Association.

Nor is that all. Rev. Jonathan Edwards, D. D., another vice-president of that Association, makes all dissenters atheists. He names atheists, deists, Jews, and Seventh-day Baptists, then classes them all together as atheists. I will read his own words : —

" These all are, for the occasion, and so far as our amendment is concerned, one class. They use the same arguments and the same tactics against us. They must be counted together, which we very much regret, but which we cannot help. The first-named is the leader in the discontent and in the outcry — the atheist, to whom nothing is higher or more sacred than man, and nothing survives the tomb. It is his class. Its labors are almost wholly in his interest ; its success would be almost wholly his triumph. The rest are adjuncts to him in this contest. They must be named from him ; **they must be treated as, for this question, one party.**"

They class us as atheists, and are going to condemn all alike ; and you are asked to give them the power. Remember these are the views of the members of the National Reform Association, whose secretary stood at this table this morning in defense of this Sunday law. These extracts show what his ideas are, and how he would use them. Dr. Everts, of Chicago, who also was here, declared last month in Chicago, in my hearing, on the subject of this Sunday law, that "it is atheism or the Sabbath."

Mr. Edwards continues : —

"What are the rights of the atheist? I would tolerate him as I would tolerate a poor lunatic ; for in my view his mind is scarcely sound. So long as he does not rave, so long as he is not dangerous, I would tolerate him. I would tolerate him as I would a conspirator. The atheist is a dangerous man. Yes, to this extent I will tolerate the atheist ; but no more. Why should I ? The atheist does not tolerate me. He does not smile either in pity or in scorn upon my faith. He hates my faith, and he hates me for my faith. . . . I can tolerate difference and discussion ; I can tolerate heresy and false religion ; I can debate the use of the Bible in our common schools, the taxation of church property, the propriety of chaplaincies and the like, but there are some questions past debate. *Tolerate atheism, sir ? There is nothing out of hell that I would not tolerate as soon !* The atheist may live, as I have said ; but, God helping us, the taint of his destructive creed shall not defile any of the civil institutions of all this fair land ! Let us repeat, atheism and Christianity are contradictory terms. They are incompatible systems. *They cannot dwell together on the same continent !*"

Senator Blair. — Many atheists are for Sunday laws.

Mr. Jones. — Let them be so if they choose ; but what I am striking at, is that these men have no right to say that I am an atheist simply because I do not believe in keeping Sunday.

Senator Blair. — You come here and seriously argue against these people, because they and the atheists blackguard each other. What have we to do with that? They abuse each other. It is worse in the Christian than in the atheist, because the Christian has some rules to guide his conduct, which the atheist has not. Here seems to be some strong intemperate language which one human being makes use of towards another. An atheist or a Christian alike may find fault with that. I do not know any way that we can interfere with it; but if you claim to argue against this bill because these people abuse atheists, I reply to that by saying that many atheists are for this bill just as these people are. They unite in support of this bill, therefore mutual recriminations amount to nothing.

Mr. Jones. — But the mutual recrimination amounts to this, that although this is confined simply to words between them now, —

Senator Blair. — I do not think you ought to argue to us by taking this precious time of yours and ours to show that these people use intemperate language towards each other.

Mr. Jones. — But I am doing it to show that they use the intemperate language now, but if they get the law, they will use more than the language against them. These men only want to make the State a party to their religious disputes. They want to get the nation by law to commit itself to the defense of religious observances, so they can add its power to their side of the controversy, and send to "hell" or some other place where the Devil is, those who even accidentally disagree with them. But the State has no business to allow itself to be made a party to any religious controversy. That has been the bane of every nation except this, and God forbid that this one should be dragged from its high estate, and made the tool of the irregular passions of religious parties. The State will find its legitimate employment in seeing that these parties keep their hands off each other, and that the ebullitions of their religious zeal are kept within the bounds of civility. It is not safe to put civil power into the hands of such men as these. But that is just what this Sunday bill will do if it shall pass.

Senator Blair. — The atheist is for this proposed law. He is not intelligently going to support a law which enables these people to burn him at the stake.

Mr. Jones. — I know he is not intelligently going to do it.

Senator Blair. — He is liable to be as intelligent as they are. Mr. Hume was a very intelligent man ; so was Voltaire ; so was Franklin, if Franklin was an atheist ; Franklin was a deist, at all events.

Mr. Jones. — It is safe to say that not one in ten of the people whose names are signed in behalf of this Sunday law know what is the intention of it, and what those will do with it when they get it.

Senator Blair. — Then it is a lack of intelligence on their part.

Mr. Jones. — I know people who signed that petition who would now be just as far from signing it as I would.

Senator Blair. — That is because you told them of those terrible consequences which they had not believed would follow. The masses of the people do not believe that the Christian people of this country have united in every State in this Union for such a purpose.

Mr. Jones. — Here is the principle : Here are six million Protestants and seven million two hundred thousand Catholics —

Senator Blair. — Cardinal Gibbons has written a letter which is in evidence. He is for it, and a great many Catholics are also for it; but it does not follow that those Catholics are for it simply because Cardinal Gibbons wrote that letter. They were for it before Cardinal Gibbons wrote the letter. You must remember that the Catholics in this country are intelligent, as well as we. Some of them are ignorant, some of us are ignorant.

Mr. Jones.—But here is the point. These people are complaining of the continental Sunday —

Senator Blair.— They do not complain of it because it is Catholic; they complain of it because it is not as good for the people as our form of Sunday.

Mr. Jones. — Certainly. And in this movement, the American Sunday, they say, comes from the Puritans, and these people know —

Senator Blair. — Do you argue against it because it comes from the Puritans, or because it comes from the Catholics? It comes from both, you say; we say it is for the good of society, and that God is for it, because it is for the good of man.

Mr. Jones. — But let me state the point that I am making: I think everybody knows that it is perfectly consistent with the Catholic keeping of Sunday for the Catholic to go to church in the morning and to the pleasure resort if he chooses in the afternoon. These men stand here in convention, and cry out against the continental Sunday and against its introduction here. Everybody knows that the continental Sunday is the Roman Catholic Sunday. Yet these men, while denouncing the continental Sunday, join hands with the Roman Catholics to secure this Sunday law. They have counted here six million Protestants and seven million two hundred thousand Catholics. Suppose this law were secured in answer to these petitions, would they then have a Puritan Sabbath, or a continental 'Sunday ?   In other words, would the six million Protestants compel the seven million two hundred thousand Catholics to keep Sunday in the Puritan, or even the Protestant way, or will the seven million two hundred thousand Catholics do as they please on Sunday, and let the six million Protestants whistle for "the breath of the Puritan" which Dr. Herrick Johnson invokes ?   More than this, if it should come to compulsion between these, would not the seven million two hundred thousand Catholics be able to make it unpleasant for the six million Protestants?

Senator Blair. — I have been all through this that the working people go through.   I have been hungry when a boy.   The first thing I can remember about is being hungry.   I know how the working people feel.   I have tugged along through the week, and been tired out Saturday night, and I have been where I would have been compelled to work to the next Monday morning if there had been no law against it.   I would not have had any chance to get that twenty-four hours of rest if the Sunday law had not given it to me.   It was a civil law under which I got it.   The masses of the working people in this country would never get that twenty-four hours' rest if there had not been a law of the land that gave it to us.   There is that practical fact, and we are fighting with that state of things.   The tired and hungry men, women, and children, all over this country, want a chance to lie down, and rest for twenty-four hours out of the whole seven days.

Mr. Jones. — So have I been through this that the working people go through.   I have carried the hod by the day.   I have swung the hammer and shoved the plane by the day.   I am a working-man now just as much as I ever was, though not in precisely the same way ; and I say to you that I never was robbed of that twenty-four hours' rest. Nor are there so many compelled to lose it as these Sunday-law advocates try to make out. Dr. Crafts said last night over in that convention that he had had communication with people in every nation but two, and —

"In the world around he could not find a man who had financially lost by refusing to work on Sunday. But many have gained by the conscientious sacrifice."

Much testimony was borne in the Chicago convention last month to the same effect in this country ; and in the convention now in session in this city, the Hon. Mr. Dingley, member of Congress from Maine, said last night that the American working-men are indifferent to the efforts which are put forth in this direction.

Senator Blair. — He is wrong about it. Mr. Dingley didn't know what he was talking about when he said that.

Mr. Jones. — He said he had investigated the matter.

Senator Blair. — I have investigated it, and I say that Mr. Dingley was simply laboring under a misapprehension.

Mr. Jones. — Dr. Crafts said this morning that he talked two hours with a convention of laboring men at Indianapolis, answering their questions, until at the end of two hours they indorsed this movement. If they are crying for it, if they are fairly tearing their hair for it, how can it be possible that he had to talk two hours to persuade them that it was all right?

Senator Blair. — Take his statement in full, if you take it at all. He says they are crying for it.

Mr. Jones. — Then why was it necessary to talk to them for two hours?

Senator Blair. — Then you simply say he did not tell the truth? You discredit the witness?

Mr. Jones. — I do.

Senator Blair. — You say perhaps he did not tell the truth, that is all. I think he was right.

Mr. Jones. — But the two things do not hitch together properly. If they are calling for it so loudly, certainly it ought not to require two hours to convert them. The fact is that the laboring men are not calling for it. Great effort is being made to have it appear so. But the Knights of Labor never took any such step except at the solicitation of Dr. Crafts. This bill had scarcely been introduced last spring before Dr. Crafts made a trip to Chicago and other cities, soliciting the indorsement of the Knights of Labor. Instead of their petitioning for this Sunday law, they have first been petitioned to petition for it ; the object of it had to be explained, and objections answered, before they could even be brought to support it. The object of the petition for this bill was explained by Dr. Crafts to the Central Labor Union of New York, and its indorsement secured. The Central Labor Union embraces a number of labor organizations, and the *Christian Union* declares the Central Labor Union to be a "radically Socialistic" organization. This, in itself, would not be particularly significant were it not for the fact that the arguments which Dr. Crafts presents to these organizations to gain their support are entirely Socialistic. Nor are these confined to Dr. Crafts. Other leaders of the movement also advocate the same principles.

Dr. Crafts went to the General Assembly of the Knights of Labor at Indianapolis last month to get the delegates there to indorse the petition for the passage of this Sunday bill. He has referred to this in his speech here this forenoon, and has made a portion of his speech to them and to the Locomotive Engineers a part of his speech here. A report of his speech at Indianapolis was printed in the *Journal of United Labor*, the official journal of the Knights of Labor of America, Thursday, Nov. 29, 1888. He said to them there : —

"Having carefully read and re-read your 'declaration of principles' and your 'constitution,' and having watched with interest the brave yet conservative shots of your *Powderly* at intemperance and other great evils, I have found myself so closely in accord with you that I have almost decided to become a Knight of Labor myself. If I do not, it will be only because I believe I can advance your 'principles' better as an outside ally."

The following question was asked by one of the Knights : —

"Would it not be the best way to stop Sunday trains to have the Government own and control the railroads altogether, as the Knights advocate?"

Dr. Crafts answered : —

"I believe in that. Perhaps the best way to begin the discussion of Government control for seven days per week is to discuss this bill for Government control on one day. If the railroads refuse the little we now ask, the people will be the more ready to take control altogether."

The Knights of Labor advocate the doctrine that the Government shall take control of all the railroads in the country, and hire the idle men in the country at regular railroad wages, and run the roads, as it now runs the Post-office Department, without reference to the question whether anything is made or lost by the Government. This is what gave rise to the above question. Dr. Crafts proposes to play into their hands by making the bid for their support, that if they will help the Sunday-law workers get Government control of the railroads one day in the week, then the Sunday-law workers will help the Knights to get Government control every day in the week.

Another question that was discussed both there and at the convention of Locomotive Engineers at Richmond, Va., was the following : —

"Will not one day's less work per week mean one-seventh less wages?"

The response to this was as follows : —

"As much railroad work as is done in seven days can be done in six days, and done better, because of the better condition of the men. And on this ground the engineers would be sustained in demanding, and, if necessary, compelling, the railroad company to so re-adjust the pay schedule that the men will be paid as much as at present."

That is to say, Dr. Crafts and the Sunday-law work-ers propose to stand in with the laboring men to com-pel employers to pay seven days' wages for six days' work. This is made certain by the following petition to the State legislatures, which is being circulated ev-erywhere with the petition for this bill. I got this at the Chicago convention. Dr. Crafts distributed the peti-tions by the quantity there, and he is doing the same at the convention now in this city : —

"*To the State Senate* [*or House*]*:* The undersigned earnestly petition your honorable body to pass a bill forbidding any one to hire another, or to be hired for more than six days in any week, except in domestic service, and the care of the sick ; in order that those whom law or custom permits to work on Sunday may be protected in their right to some other weekly rest-day, and in their right to a week's wages for six days' work."

Now a week consists of seven days. A week's wages for six days' work is seven days' wages for six days' work. This petition asks the legislatures of all the States to pass a law protecting employees in their *right* to seven days' wages for six days' work. No man in this world has any right to seven days' wages for six days' work. If he has a right to seven days' wages for six days' work, then he has an equal right to six days'

wages for five days' work ; and to five days' wages for
four days' work ; and to four days' wages for three days'
work ; to three days' wages for two days' work ; to
two days' wages for one day's work ; and to one day's
wages for no work at all. This is precisely what the
proposition amounts to. For in proposing to pay seven
days' wages for six days' work, it does propose to pay
one day's wages for no work. But if a man is entitled
to one day's wages for doing nothing, why stop with
one day ? Why not go on and pay him full wages every
day for doing nothing ? It may be thought that I mis-
interpret the meaning of the petition ; that, as it asks
that nobody be allowed to hire another for more than
six days of any week, it may mean only that six days
are to compose a week ; and that it is a week's wages of
six days only that is to be paid for six days' work.
That is *not* the meaning of the petition. It is not the
intention of those who are gaining the support of the
Knights of Labor by inventing and circulating the
petition.

Dr. George Elliott, pastor of the Foundry Metho-
dist Church in this city, — the church in which this National Sunday Convention is being held, — the church
that is now festooned with fourteen million petitions
that they have n't got, — festooned, at least partly, with
one seven-million-two-hundred-thousand-times-multi-
plied Cardinal, — Dr. Elliott, while speaking in favor of
this bill this forenoon, was asked by Senator Call these
questions : —

" Do you propose that Congress shall make provision
to pay the people in the employ of the Government who
are exempted on Sunday, for Sunday work ? "

" *Mr. Elliott.* — I expect you to give them adequate
compensation.

" *Senator Call.* — Do you propose that the same
amount shall be paid for six days' work as for seven ?

" *Mr. Elliott.* — I do ; for the reason that we believe these employees can do all the work that is to be done in six days. And if they do all the work, they ought to have all the pay."

There it is in plain, unmistakable words, that they deliberately propose to have laws, State and national, which shall compel employers to pay seven days' wages for six days' work. This is sheer Socialism ; it is the very essence of Socialism. No wonder they gained the unanimous indorsement of the convention of the Knights of Labor, and of the Locomotive Engineers, and the Socialistic Labor Union of New York City, by proposing to pay them good wages for doing nothing. I confess that I, too, would support the bill upon such a proposition as that *if I looked no further than the money that is in it.*

But this is not all. The Knights of Labor not only accept the proposition, but they carry it farther, and logically, too. This principle has been advocated for some time by the Knights of Labor in demanding ten hours' pay for eight hours' work — virtually two hours' pay for doing nothing. The *Christian Union* and the *Catholic Review* propose to help the working-men secure their demanded eight-hour law, and then have the working-men help to get the six-day law by forbidding all work on Sunday. Dr. Crafts and Dr. Elliott go a step farther, and propose to secure the support of the working-men by having laws enacted compelling employers to pay them full wages on Sunday for doing nothing. But the Knights of Labor do not propose to stop with this. The same copy of the *Journal of United Labor* which contained the speech of Dr. Crafts, contained the following in an editorial upon this point : —

" Why should not such a law be enacted ? All the work now performed each week could easily be accomplished in five days of eight hours each if employment were given to the host of willing idle men who are now walking the streets. It is a crime to force one portion of a community to kill themselves by overwork, while another portion of the same people are suffering from privation and hunger, with no opportunity to labor. The speech of the Rev. Mr. Crafts, published elsewhere, furnishes an abundance of argument as to why such a law should be put in force."

So when the Sunday-law advocates propose to pay a week's wages for six days' work of eight hours each, because all the work can be done in six days that is now done in seven, then the Knights of Labor propose to have a week's wages for five days' work, because, by employing all the idle men, all the work that is now done in seven days can be done in five. And as Dr. Elliott has said, " If they do all the work, they ought to have all the pay." But if a week's wages are to be paid for five days' work of eight hours each, that is to say, if two days' wages can rightly be paid for no work at all, why should the thing be stopped there? If the Government is to take control of the railroads all the time in order to pay two days' wages for doing nothing, and if the States are to enact laws compelling employers to pay employees two days' wages for doing nothing, then why shall not the Government, both State and national, take possession of everything, and pay the laboring men full wages all the time for doing nothing? For if men have the right to one day's wages for no work, where is the limit to the exercise of that right? The fact of the matter is that there is no limit. If a man is entitled to wages for doing nothing part of the time, he is entitled to wages for doing nothing all the time. And the principle upon which Dr. Crafts and his other Sunday-law *confrères* gain the support of the working-men to this Sunday bill is nothing at all but the principle of downright Socialism.

There is a point right here that is worthy of the serious consideration of the working-men. These Sunday-law workers profess great sympathy for the laboring men in their struggle with the grinding monopolies, and by Sunday laws they propose to deliver the working-men from the power of these monopolies. But in the place of all these other monopolies, they propose to establish a *monopoly of religion*, and to have the Government secure them in the perpetual enjoyment of it. They may talk as much as they please about the grasping, grinding greed of the many kinds of monopolies, and there is truth in it ; but of all monopolies, the most greedy, the most grinding, the most oppressive, the most conscienceless the world ever saw or ever can see, is a religious monopoly. When these managers of religious legislation have delivered the working-men from the other monopolies — granting that they can do it — then the important question is, Who will deliver the working-men from the religious monopoly ?

Senator Blair. — Abolish the law of rest, take it away from the working people, and leave corporations and saloon keepers and everybody at perfect liberty to destroy that twenty-four hours of rest, and lawgivers and law-makers will find out whether or not the people want it, and whether they want those law-makers.

Mr. Jones. — There are plenty of ways to help the working-men without establishing a religious monopoly, and enforcing religious observance upon all. There is another point that comes in right here. Those who are asking for the law and those who work for it, are those who compel the people to work on Sunday. In the Illinois State Sunday convention in Chicago last month, it was stated in the first speech made in the convention, "We remember how that the working-men are compelled to desecrate the Sabbath by the great corporations." The very next sentence was, "We remember also that the stockholders, the owners of these railroads, are members of the churches, that they sit in the pews and bow their heads in the house of God on the Sabbath day."

Senator Blair. — That is only saying that there are hypocrites in this world. What has that to do with this proposed law?

Mr. Jones. — I am coming to that. It has a good deal to do with it. The stockholders who own the railroads act in this way, those men said ; and it was stated by a minister in that convention that a railroad president told him that there were more petitions for Sunday trains from preachers than from any other class.

Senator Blair. — There are a lot of hypocrites among the preachers, then.

Mr. Jones. — Precisely ; although you yourself have said it. I confess I have not the heart to dispute it.

Senator Blair. — I do not find any fault with that statement. If it is true, it does not touch this question.

Mr. Jones. — If these preachers and church members will not keep the Sabbath in obedience to what they say is the commandment of God, will they keep it in obedience to the command of the State?

Senator Blair. — Certainly the hard working man needs rest ; the preachers, church members, and millionaires may do as they please : the bill comes in here and says that the national government, taking part of the jurisdiction of the civil government of the United States by a concession made by the States, by virtue of its control of interstate commerce, and the post-office business, and the army and navy, will take advantage of what the States have given to the general Government in the way of jurisdiction, and will not introduce practices which destroy the Sabbath in the States. That is the object of this legislation. That is all that is under-

8

taken here. It is simply an act proposing to make efficient the Sunday-rest laws of the State, and nothing else.

Mr. Jones. — But those laws are to be enforced, if at all, by those who are so strongly in favor of them.

Senator Blair. — No, by the State. If these people were in favor of them, or not in favor of them, or violated them, that is another thing. A man may be for a law which he violates. A great many of the strongest temperance people in the world use intoxicating liquors. They say that they realize the evil, and that they are in favor of the enactment of law which will extirpate those evils. The strongest advocates I have ever seen of temperance legislation are men who have come to realize that the grave is just ahead of them. They cannot get rid of the appetite, but they pray the Government for legislation that will save the boys.

Mr. Jones. — That is all right. I am in favor of prohibition straight ; but not Sunday prohibition.

Senator Blair. — You cannot adduce a man's practice as a reply to the argument on a question that touches the public good. It does not vitiate a man's principle because he fails to live up to it himself.

Mr. Jones. — But the secret of the whole matter is this : As an argument for the Sunday law, these men assert that the great railroad corporations desecrate the Sabbath, and by persistently running Sunday trains, also compel the railroad men to work and to desecrate the day. They at the same time assert that the men who own the railroads belong to the churches. If, then, the railroads compel their men to desecrate the day, and the owners of the railroads are church members, then who is it but the church members that are compelling people to desecrate the day ?

Further than this, they quoted at Chicago the statement of a railroad president, that the roads "get more requests for Sunday trains signed by preachers" than they do from other people. But as the church members own the railroads, and the preachers request them to run Sunday trains, then who is to blame for the "desecration" of the day but the preachers and their own church members ? Can't the preachers stop asking for Sunday trains without being compelled to do so by the civil law ? In the Chicago convention last month — November 20, 21 — Dr. Knowles, who is secretary of this National Sunday-law Union, said that by the influence of William E. Dodge, even after his death, the Delaware & Lackawanna Railroad Company had resisted the temptation to run trains on Sunday until the present year. But five hundred ministers met in conference in New York and used competing lines on Sunday, and by this the hands of the Sunday observance committee have been tied ever since. After that, when the Delaware & Lackawanna directors were asked not to run Sunday trains, they replied, —

"How can you come to us pleading for us to run no trains on Sunday, when your preachers by the hundreds on Sunday use our rival lines, which do run on Sunday. If your preachers ride on Sunday trains on other roads, we cannot see why they and other people cannot ride on our trains on Sunday. And if it is all right for these other roads to run trains on Sunday, — and certainly ministers of the gospel would not ride on them if it were wrong, — then we cannot see how it can be such a great wrong for us to run Sunday trains."

That is a very proper answer. No wonder the Sunday committee's hands are tied by it. And yet that very conference of five hundred preachers, assembled in New York last summer, took the first decided step toward the organization of the National Sunday Association, of which Dr. Knowles himself is secretary.

By these facts there is presented the following condition of things: (1.) Church members own the railroads; (2.) Preachers sign requests for Sunday trains; (3.) The church members grant the request of the preachers for Sunday trains, and the preachers ride on the Sunday trains, and other church members go on Sunday excursions; (4.) Then the whole company — preachers and church members — together petition Congress and the State legislatures to make a law stopping all Sunday trains! That is to say, they want the legislatures, State and national, to compel their own railroad-owning church members not to grant the request of the preachers for Sunday trains. In other words, they want the civil power to compel them all — preachers and church members — to act as they all say that Christians ought to act. And they insist upon quoting all the time the commandment of God, "Remember the Sabbath day to keep it holy." But if they will not obey the commandment of God, which they themselves acknowledge and quote, what assurance have we that they will obey the law of Congress or State legislature when they get it, especially as it will rest entirely with themselves to see that the law is enforced? Will they compel themselves by civil law to do what they themselves will not otherwise do? The sum of this whole matter is that they want the civil power to enforce church discipline; and that not only upon themselves, but upon everybody else. The whole system, and all the pretensions upon which this Sunday law is demanded, are crooked.

As to the enforcement of the law, it will fall to those who are working to get it; because certainly those who do not want it will not enforce it, and the officers of the law are not given to the enforcement of laws which are not supported by public opinion. This is proved by the fact that the State of Illinois and the city of Chicago now have Sunday laws that ought to satisfy any reasonable person, and yet not one of them is enforced. And the preachers of that city and State, instead of seeing that these are enforced, call convention after convention to work up more Sunday laws, both State and national.

What, then, is the next intention? — It is to make it a political question in both State and nation, and make the enactment and enforcement of Sunday laws the price of votes and political support. This is proved by the following resolutions adopted by the Elgin Sunday-law convention : —

"*Resolved*, That we look with shame and sorrow on the non-observance of the Sabbath by many Christian people, in that the custom prevails with them of purchasing Sabbath newspapers, engaging in and patronizing Sabbath business and travel, and in many instances giving themselves to pleasure and self-indulgence, setting aside by neglect and indifference the great duties and privileges which God's day brings them.

"*Resolved*, That we give our votes and support to those candidates or political officers who will pledge themselves to vote for the enactment and enforcing of statutes in favor of the civil Sabbath."

Such a resolution as this last may work in Illinois, though it is doubtful, but with their own statement made in that convention, it is certain that this resolution can never work under the Constitution of the United States. They stated in the convention that the Sabbath is "the test of all religion." To demand that candidates or political officers shall pledge themselves to vote for the enactment and enforcement of statutes in favor of the Sabbath is, therefore, to require a religious test as a qualification for office. The national Constitution declares that "no religious test shall ever be required as a qualification to any office or public trust under this Government ;" consequently, no Sabbath or Sunday-law test can ever be applied to any candidate for any national office or public trust.

It is true they use the word *civil* in the resolution, but that corresponds with much of their other work. There is not, and there cannot be, any such thing as a *civil* Sabbath. The Sabbath is religious wholly, and they know it; and in all their discussion of this resolution and the subject generally in the convention, it was as a religious institution, and that only.

Senator Blair. — Is there any other point you would wish to present?

Mr. Jones. — There is another point, and that is, that we will be sufferers under such a law when it is passed. They propose to put in an exemption clause. Some of them favor an exemption clause, but it would not in the least degree check our opposition to the law if forty exemption clauses were put in, unless, indeed, they should insert a clause exempting *everybody* who does not want to keep it. In that case, we might not object so much.

Senator Blair. — You care not whether it is put in or not?

Mr. Jones. — There is no right whatever in the legislation; and we will never accept an exemption clause as an equivalent to our opposition to the law. It is not to obtain relief for ourselves that we oppose the law. It is the principle of the whole subject of the legislation to which we object; and an exemption clause would not modify our objection in the least.

Senator Blair. — You differ from Dr. Lewis?

Mr. Jones. — Yes, sir, we will never accept an exemption clause, as tending in the least to modify our opposition to the law. We as firmly and as fully deny the right of the State to legislate upon the subject with an exemption clause as without.

Senator Blair. — There are three times as many of you as of his denomination?

Mr. Jones. — Yes, sir ; there are nearly thirty thousand of us, and we ask for no exemption clause. We stand wholly upon the principle of the question. There should be no exemption from a just law. If the law is right, it is wrong to exempt.

In 1887 Mrs. Bateham herself wrote and printed a "Letter to Seventh-day Believers," proposing in substance that if we would help them to secure a Sunday law, they would exempt us from its penalties. We replied then as we reply now and always. We will not help you to put upon others what we would not have put upon ourselves.

Senator Blair. — You object to it ?

Mr. Jones. — We object to the whole principle of the proposed legislation. We go to the root of the matter, and deny the right of Congress to enact it.

Senator Blair. — You say that the proposed exemption does not make it any better ?

Mr. Jones. — Not a bit ; because if the rightfulness of the legislation be admitted, then we admit that it is the right of a majority to say that such and such a day shall be the Sabbath or the Lord's day, and that it shall be kept. The majorities change in civil government ; the majority may change within a few years, — may change, in fact, at any election, — and then the people may say that the day which we believe should be kept must be observed, or they may say that this day shall not be kept. If we admit the propriety of the legislation, we must also admit the propriety of the legislation to the effect that a certain day shall not be kept, and it makes every man's observance of Sunday, or otherwise, simply the football of majorities. That has been the course of religious legislation from the formation of the papacy onward, and that is the end of religious legislation of all kinds everywhere.

Senator Blair. — Do you not think there is a distinction between a majority in a monarchical government, and a majority in a republican government? In a monarchical government the majority is simply one man who has power.

Mr. Jones. — But in a republic when you throw this subject into civil affairs, it makes a great deal of difference. Why, sir, we would object to the passage of a law enforcing the observance of the day which we keep, and to accept an exemption clause would only be to contradict ourselves. Allow me to illustrate this: There was a time when we did not keep the seventh day as the Sabbath. While we did not keep it, we had the right not to keep it. We became convinced that we ought to keep it; and we are now doing so. We have the right to keep it. More than this, we have the right again not to keep it if we choose not to keep it. But if, while keeping it, we should consent to the State's assumption of power to compel us to do that which we have the right to omit if we please, we would therein resign our freedom of religious faith and worship. If these people would only *think* on this question, they would see that they themselves cannot afford to consent to this legislation, much less demand it. No man can ever safely consent to legislation in favor of the form of faith or worship which he himself professes. In so doing he resigns his right to profess some other form of faith if he should become convinced that that other form is nearer the truth than his own. He virtually resigns his right to think any further on the subject of religious observances, and must thenceforth accept them ready made from the legislative power; that is, as the majority may dictate. The Sunday observers may thus give away their religious liberty if they choose; but as for us, we do not propose to do it. We are going to assert and maintain our rights. And when these give theirs away, we are going to assert their right to re-assert their rights.

Another thing: An exemption clause is only a toleration clause in disguise. For us to accept it would be but to confess that all religious rights are summed up in the majority, and that we are willing to accept from *them* whatever religious liberty *they* think we ought to have. But no such confession, sir, will we ever make. To no such thing will we ever consent or submit. We are Americans, sir, and citizens of the United States, too, and we assert all the rights of American citizens. The vocabulary of American ideas knows no such word as "toleration." It asserts *rights*. As was said by the Senate Committee on this very subject sixty years ago, so say we, —

"*What other nations call religious toleration, we call religious rights. They are not exercised by virtue of governmental indulgence, but as rights, of which government cannot deprive any portion of citizens, however small. Despotic power may invade those rights, but justice still confirms them.*"

Nor is this all that there is to be said on this point. There is another principle involved. If we should accept the exemption clause, it would not help the thing. It would be exceedingly short. Suppose an exemption clause were given. There are people who would profess to be Seventh-day Adventists for the express purpose of getting a chance to open saloons or houses of business on Sunday. Therefore in outright self-defense, the majority would have to repeal the exemption clause.

Senator Blair. — Call Mrs. Bateham's attention to that.

Mr. Jones. — Let me repeat it. If you give an exemption clause — it has been tried — there are reprehensible men, saloon keepers, who know they will get more traffic on Sunday than they can on Saturday, and they will profess to be Seventh-day Adventists, they will profess to be Sabbath keepers. You cannot "go behind the returns," you cannot look into the heart, you cannot investigate the intention, to see whether they are genuine in their profession or not. They will profess to be Sabbath keepers, and then they will open their saloons on Sunday. Then in outright self-defense, to make your position effective, you will have to repeal that exemption clause. It will last but a little while.

Senator Blair. — I agree with you there.

Mr. Jones. — For that reason these people **cannot** afford to offer an exemption clause ; and for the reason that it puts the majority in the power of our conscience, we deny the right to do anything of the kind. I ask the organizations represented here to think of this after this hearing is over. It will bear all the investigation they choose to give it.

Senator Blair. — I should like to call everybody's attention to the point. If you need any legislation of this kind, you would better ask for legislation to carry out your purposes, and be careful that in the effort to get the assistance of the parties against you, you do not throw away the pith and substance of all for which you ask.

Mr. Jones. — Yes, sir, that is the point. To show the workings of this principle, I will state that Arkansas in 1885 had an exemption clause in its Sunday law. That exemption clause, it was claimed, was taken advantage of by saloon keepers to keep open on Sunday. A delegation went to the legislature of Arkansas, and asked them to repeal the exemption clause, so that they could shut the saloons on Sunday. The legislature did it. If they had shut the saloons on Sunday, that would have been all well enough. But they did not even try it. There was not a saloon keeper arrested under that repealed law ; there were only two men not keeping the seventh day, who were arrested under it; there was not a man who did not keep the seventh day fined under it; but there were Seventh-day Baptists and some Seventh-day Adventists, poor almost as Job's turkey, who were prosecuted and fined. One man had his only horse taken from him, and his cow, and at last his brethren contributed money to save him from jail. Such men were prosecuted time and again; and the lawyers of the State, under the leadership of Senator Crockett, succeeded in carrying through the legislature, against the persistent opposition of the church mana-·gers, a bill restoring the exemption clause, to save these poor, innocent people from the persecution that was being carried on.*

Senator Blair. — I am glad you put in that fact, because it is something that happened.

Mr. Jones. — I ask leave to read the statement made in the Arkansas Legislature by Senator Crockett, upon that very subject: —

"Let me, sir, illustrate the operation of the present law by one or two examples. A Mr. Swearigen came from a Northern State and settled on a farm in —— County. His farm was four miles from town, and far away from any house of religious worship. He was a member of the Seventh-day Adventist Church, and, after having sacredly observed the Sabbath of his people (Saturday) by abstaining from all secular work, he and his son, a lad of seventeen, on the first day of the week went quietly about their usual avocations. They disturbed no one — interfered with the rights of no one. But they were observed, and reported to the Grand Jury, indicted, arrested, tried, convicted, fined, and having no

---

* Yet in the very next legislature, that of 1889, the church managers tried their best again to repeal the exemption clause. It was then discovered that they had elected men to the legislature pledged to repeal the exemption clause. The bill passed the Senate, but was killed in the House. This proves my position, that there is no liberty in an exemption clause.

money to pay the fine, these moral, Christian citizens of Arkansas were dragged to the county jail and imprisoned like felons for twenty-five days—and for what? —For daring, in this so-called land of liberty, in the year of our Lord 1887, to worship God.

"Was this the end of the story?—Alas, no, sir! They were turned out; and the old man's only horse, his sole reliance to make bread for his children, was levied on to pay the fine and costs, amounting to thirty-eight dollars. The horse sold at auction for twenty-seven dollars. A few days afterward the sheriff came again, and demanded thirty-six dollars, eleven dollars balance due on fine and costs, and twenty-five dollars for board for himself and son while in jail. And when the poor old man—a Christian, mind you—told him with tears that he had no money, he promptly levied on his only cow, but was persuaded to accept bond, and the amount was paid by contributions from his friends of the same faith. Sir, my heart swells to bursting with indignation as I repeat to you the infamous story.

"Another, and I am done. Sir, I beg you and these senators to believe that these are neither fancy nor exaggerated sketches. Five years ago a young man, newly married, came to ——— County from Ohio. He and his wife were Seventh-day Baptists. The young girl had left father and mother, brothers and sisters, and all the dear friends of her childhood, to follow her young husband to Arkansas—to them the land of promise. The light of love sparkled in her bright young eyes. The roses of health were upon her cheeks, and her silvery laugh was sweet music, of which her young husband never wearied. They purchased a little farm, and soon by tireless industry and frugal thrift, their home blossomed like a rose in the wilderness. After awhile a fair young babe came to them to brighten the sunshine, and sweeten the bird songs. They were happy in each other's affection and their love for the little one. For them 'all things worked together for good;' for in their humble, trusting way, they worshiped God and loved their fellow-men.

"Two years ago the law under which their prosperity and happiness had had its growth was repealed!

Accursed be the day which brought such a foul blot
upon our State's fair fame! A change, sudden, cold, and
blasting as an Arctic storm, came over their lives, and
pitilessly withered all their bright flowers of hope.
Under this repeal, persecution lifted its ugly, venomous
head. The hero of my sad story was observed by an
envious, jealous neighbor, quietly working, as he believed
God had commanded him, on Sunday. He was reported
to that Inquisitorial relic of barbarism, the Grand Jury,
indicted, tried, convicted, and thrown into jail because
his conscience would not let him pay the fine.

"Week after week dragged its slow length along.
Day after day the young wife, with baby in her arms,
watched at the gate for his coming, and, like Tenny-
son's Marianna —

> "'She only said : "My life is dreary —
> He cometh not," she said.
> She said : "I am aweary — aweary —
> I would that I were dead."'

"Then baby sickened and died; the light in the
young wife's eyes faded out in tears ; her silvery laugh
changed to low, wailing sobs. Pale-faced Misery snatched
the roses from her cheeks, and planted in their stead
her own pallid hue. Sir, how can I go on? At length
the cruel law was appeased, and this inoffensive citizen
(except that he had loved God and sought to obey him)
was released from prison, and dragged his weary feet to
the happy home he had left a few short weeks before.
He met his neighbors at the gate bearing a coffin. He
asked no questions, his heart told him all. No, not all!
He knew not — he could never know — of her lonely
hours, of her bitter tears, of the weary watching and
waiting, of the appeals to God, — that God for whom she
had suffered so much, — for help in the hour of her extrem-
ity, of baby's sickness and death. He could not know
of these. But he went with them to the quiet country
burial-place, and saw beside the open grave a little
mound with dirt freshly heaped upon it, and then he
knew that God had taken both his heart's idols, and he
was left alone. His grief was too deep for tears. With
staring eyes, he saw them lower the body of his young

wife into the grave. He heard the clods rattle upon the
coffin, and it seemed as if they were falling upon his
heart. The work was done, and they left him with his
dead ; and then he threw himself down between the
graves, with an arm across each little mound, and the
tears came in torrents, and kept his heart from breaking.
And then he sobbed his broken farewell to his darlings,
and left Arkansas forever, — left it, sir, as hundreds of
others are preparing to leave, if this General Assembly
fails to restore to them the protection of their rights
under the Constitution, national and State.

"On next Monday, at Malvern, six as honest, good,
and virtuous citizens as live in Arkansas, are to be tried
as criminals for daring to worship God in accordance
with the dictates of their own consciences ; for exercising a right which this Government, under the Constitution, has no power to abridge. Sir, I plead, in the
name of justice, in the name of our republican institutions, in the name of these inoffensive, God-fearing,
God-serving people, our fellow-citizens, and last, sir, in
the name of Arkansas, I plead that this bill may pass,
and this one foul blot be wiped from the escutcheon of
our glorious commonwealth."

Arkansas was not alone in this, however, though it
was worse there than anywhere else. I myself, with
other brethren in California, had to send hundreds of
dollars into Tennessee, to support the families of the
brethren of our own faith there, while the husbands and
fathers who made the money for their support were in
jail because they chose to work for their families on Sunday, and make bread for them after having kept the
Sabbath according to their conscience. That has been
done, Mr. Chairman, in these United States. That is
the care these people have for the laboring man.

Senator Blair. — You reason from that that there
should be no Sunday law whatever?

Mr. Jones. — If you allow a Sunday law, you must
allow it to any extent. It must be enforced. All they

did in Arkansas was to enforce the law, simply as in the Roman empire they enforced the law, and put Christians to death. They simply enforced the law, but the law was wrong. Any condition of the law that will allow such things as that is a wrong condition of the law.

Senator Blair. — This bill proposes that work must not be done to the disturbance of others. This work was done to the disturbance of others.

Mr. Jones. — I know that this bill for a national Sunday law proposes that work must not be done "to the disturbance of others," and in that very phrase lies one of its worst features. The bill declares that no person shall do any work, or "engage in any play, game, or amusement, or recreation, to the disturbance of others, on the first day of the week, commonly known as the Lord's day, or during any part thereof." This leaves it entirely with the other man to say whether that which I do disturbs him ; and that is only to make every man's action on Sunday subject to the whim or caprice of his neighbor. And everybody knows that it requires a very slight thing to disturb one who has a spite or prejudice against you. At the Illinois State Sunday-law convention last month (Nov. 20, 21), Dr. R. O. Post, of Springfield, made a speech on the subject of "Sunday Recreation," in which he declared as the sum of his whole speech that, —

"There is no kind of recreation that is proper or •profitable on Sunday, outside of the home or the sanctuary."

Only let such a law as is embodied in this bill become of force where R. O. Post, D. D., is, and any kind of recreation outside of the home or the sanctuary would be sure to disturb him, and the one engaged in the recreation could be arrested and prosecuted. But it may be argued that no judge or jury would uphold any such prosecution. That is not at all certain, as we shall

yet see ; but whether or not it is so, it is certain that if
your neighbor should say that what you did disturbed
him, under such a law as that he could have you arrested, and put to the inconvenience and expense of
defending yourself before the court.   In 1887, the city
of San Francisco, Cal., had an ordinance on another
subject that embodied the very principle of this clause
of this Sunday bill.   It reads thus : —

"No person shall in any place indulge in conduct
having a tendency to annoy persons passing or being
upon the public highway, or upon adjacent premises."

It is easy to see that the principle of this ordinance
is identical with that of the clause in the first section of
this bill, which forbids anything "to the disturbance of
others."

While that San Francisco ordinance was in force, a
man by the name of Ferdinand Pape was distributing
some circulars on the street, which not only had a tendency to annoy, but actually "annoyed" a business
man across the street.   Pape was arrested.   He applied
to the Superior Court for a writ of *habeas corpus*, claiming that the offense charged against him did not constitute a crime, and that the ordinance making such action
an offense was invalid and void, because it was unreasonable and uncertain.   The report of the case says : —

"The writ was made returnable before Judge Sul-
livan, and argued by Henry Hutton in behalf of the imprisoned offender.   Disposing of the question, the Judge
gave quite a lengthy written opinion, in which he passed
a somewhat severe criticism upon the absurdity of the
contested ordinance, and discharged Pape from custody.
Said the Judge : —

"'If the order be law, enforceable by fine and imprisonment, it is a crime to indulge in any conduct, however innocent and harmless in itself, and however un-
consciously done, which has a tendency to annoy other

persons. . . . Instances might be multiplied indefinitely in which the most harmless and inoffensive conduct has a tendency to annoy others. If the language of the ordinance defines a criminal offense, it sets a very severe penalty of liberty and property upon conduct lacking in the essential element of criminality.

"'But it may be said that courts and juries will not use the instrumentality of this language to set the seal of condemnation on unoffending citizens, and to unjustly deprive them of their liberty and brand them as criminals. The law countenances no such dangerous doctrine, countenances no principle so subversive of liberty, as that the life or liberty of a subject should be made to depend upon the whim or caprice of judge or jury, by exercising a discretion in determining that certain conduct does or does not come within the inhibition of a criminal action. The law should be engraved so plainly and distinctly on the legislative tables that it can be discerned alike by all subjects of the commonwealth, whether judge upon the bench, juror in the box, or prisoner at the bar. Any condition of the law which allows the test of criminality to depend on the whim or caprice of judge or juror, savors of tyranny. The language employed is broad enough to cover conduct which is clearly within the Constitutional rights of the citizen. It designates no border-line which divides the criminal from the non-criminal conduct. Its terms are too vague and uncertain to lay down a rule of conduct. In my judgment, the portion of the ordinance here involved is uncertain and unreasonable.'"

This decision applies with full force to this proposed national Sunday law. Under this law, all that would be necessary to subject any person to a criminal prosecution, would be for him to engage in any sort of play, game, amusement, or recreation on Sunday; because the National Reformers are as much in favor of this Sunday law as is anybody else, and there are many of those rigid National Reformers who would be very much "disturbed" by any amusement or recreation indulged in on

Sunday, however innocent it might be in itself. And it is left entirely to the whim or caprice of the "disturbed" one, or of the judge or jury, to say whether the action really has or has not disturbed him.

The California decision is, that such a statute "sets a very severe penalty of liberty and property upon conduct lacking in the essential element of criminality." California courts "countenance no such dangerous doctrine, countenance no principle so subversive of liberty," or which so "savors of tyranny," as that which is embodied in these words of this Sunday bill.

Nor is this confined to this particular section; the same principle is found in Section 5. This section provides that if any person works for any other person on Sunday, and receives payment for it at any time, then any person in the wide world, except the parties concerned, can enter suit, and recover the money so paid. If you work for me on Sunday, and I pay you for it, then the first man that finds it out can sue you and get the money. That is what the bill says. When wages are paid for Sunday work, "whether in advance or otherwise, the same may be recovered back by *whoever* shall *first* sue for the same." *Whoever* is a universal term. Therefore, this bill deliberately proposes that when any man who is subject to the exclusive jurisdiction of the United States, receives payment for work done on Sunday, except for work of necessity or mercy, he may be sued for that money by whoever first learns that he has received it, and that person shall get the money.

So much for this bill as it reads. Now, as to the work for which the Seventh-day observers of Arkansas were prosecuted. It was not to the disturbance of others. Let me state some of the facts, the authentic record of which I have, but it is too voluminous to present in detail.

With two exceptions, all the arrests and prosecutions were of people who observed the seventh day of the week as the Sabbath. And in these two exceptions, those who were held for trial were held without bail, — simply on their own recognizance, — and although the testimony was direct and positive, the jury "agreed to disagree," and the cases were both dismissed; while in every case of a Seventh-day Adventist, the least bail that was accepted was $110; the most of them were held under bonds for $250, and some for as high as $500. There was not a single case dismissed, and in all the cases the complaint was never made that what was done had disturbed the worship or the rest of any one. But the indictments were all for the crime of "Sabbath-breaking" by the performance of labor on Sunday.

The statute of Arkansas at that time ran thus : —

"SECTION 1883. Every person who shall on the Sabbath, or Sunday, be found laboring, or shall compel his apprentice or servant to labor or perform service other than customary household duties of daily necessity, comfort, or charity, on conviction thereof shall be fined one dollar for each separate offense.

"SEC. 1884. Every apprentice or servant compelled to labor on Sunday shall be deemed a separate offense of the master.

"SEC. 1885. The provision of this act shall not apply to steamboats and other vessels navigating the waters of the State, nor such manufacturing establishments as require to be kept in continual operation."

In the case of Mr. Swearingen, mentioned by Senator Crockett, the conviction was upon the testimony of a witness who swore that the work for which he was convicted was done on a day which proved to be *seventeen days before the law was enacted*, thus by its enforcement making the law *ex post facto*. The Constitution of the United States forbids the making of *ex post facto* laws. But when a law not being *ex post facto* in itself, is made so by its enforcement, it is time that something was being done to enlighten courts and juries upon that subject, even though it should be by an amendment to the Constitution of the United States, providing that no law not being *ex post facto* in itself shall be made so by its enforcement. Then, on the other hand, several cases were tried, and the men convicted and fined *after the law was repealed*, though for work done before.

In almost every case the informer, the prosecuting witness, or perhaps both, were men who were doing work or business on the same day, and sometimes with the very persons accused; yet the man who kept the seventh day was convicted in every instance, while the man who did not keep the seventh day, but did work or business with the man who did, was left entirely unmolested, and his evidence was accepted in Court to convict the other man. I give some instances: —

First, a man by the name of Millard Courtney, who was the prosecuting witness against two men, Armstrong and Elmore, had taken a man with him to where these men were working, and there they made a contract for roofing a school-house; and yet Courtney's evidence convicted these two men of Sabbath-breaking at the very time he was doing business with them.

Second, J. L. Shockey was convicted upon the testimony of a man by the name of Hammond, who went to him on Sunday where he was at work, and bargained with him for a Plymouth Rock rooster.

Third, J. L. James, who worked in the rain for nothing on Sunday that a poor widow, a member of another church, might be sheltered, was convicted of Sabbath breaking upon the evidence of a man who carried wood and chopped it up that same day within seven rods of the man who was convicted by his testimony.

Fourth, one La Fever and his wife went to Allen Meeks's house on Sunday to visit. They found Meeks planting potatoes. Meeks stopped planting potatoes, and spent the rest of the day visiting with them ; and yet Meeks was convicted of Sabbath-breaking and fined upon the evidence of La Fever.

Fifth, the second case of Mr. Meeks. Riley Warren went to his house on Sunday, to see him about hiring a teacher for the public school. In the social, neighborly conversation that passed between them, Meeks incidentally mentioned that he had mended his wagon-brake that morning ; and yet he was convicted of Sabbath-breaking upon the evidence of that same Riley Warren. Meeks was thus virtually compelled to be a witness against himself, — clearly another violation of both the State and United States Constitution.

Sixth, Mr. Reeves's boys were hauling wood on Sunday. In the timber where they got the wood, they met another boy, a Seventh-day Adventist, John A. Meeks, hunting squirrels. They joined him in the hunt, scaring the squirrels around the trees so he could shoot them. Then the squirrels were divided between the Meeks boy and the Reeves boys. Then the Meeks boy was indicted, prosecuted, and convicted of Sabbath-breaking upon the evidence of the father of those boys who were hauling wood, and who helped to kill the squirrels.

Seventh, James M. Pool, for hoeing in his garden on Sunday, was convicted of Sabbath-breaking, on the evidence of a "sanctified" church member who had gone to Pool's house on Sunday to buy tobacco.

Allow me to mention the methods of prosecution. In the case of Scoles, J. A. Armstrong was called before the Grand Jury. After repeated answers to questions in regard to work done on Sunday by different parties in several different lines of business and traffic, he was asked the direct question whether he knew of any Seventh-day Adventists who worked on

Sunday, and when in the nature of the case he answered in the affirmative, every one of the Seventh-day Adventists whom he named was indicted, and not one of any other class or trade.

In the second case of James A. Armstrong; he was arrested at the instance of the mayor. When asked for the affidavit upon which Armstrong was arrested, the mayor said that A. J. Vaughn had called his attention to Armstrong's working, and had said, "Now see that you do your duty," yet Vaughn testified under oath that he did not see Armstrong at all on the day referred to. Armstrong was not only arrested at the instance of the mayor, but he was also tried before the mayor, who acted as Justice of the Peace. And when Vaughn testified that he had not seen Armstrong at all on the day referred to, this made the mayor, virtually, both prosecuting witness and judge; and the questions which he asked show that that was precisely his position, and his own view of the case. The question which he asked to each of the first two witnesses was, "What do you know about Mr. Armstrong's working on Sunday, June 27?" This question assumes all that was expected to be proved on the trial.

This is enough to show the workings of such a Sunday law as is embodied in this Senate bill. There were many other cases, every one in the same line. But throughout the whole list of cases, it is only the record of how people who were performing honest labor on their own premises in a way in which it was impossible to do harm to any soul on earth, were indicted, prosecuted, and convicted upon the evidence of men who, if there were any wrong involved in the case at all, were more guilty than they. If religious persecution could possibly be more clearly demonstrated than it is in this thing, we hope never to see an illustration of it.

It may be asked, Why was not an appeal taken? An appeal was taken to the Supreme Court of the

State, in the first case that was tried. The judgment of the lower Court was confirmed in an opinion closing with these words : —

"The appellant's argument, then, is reduced to this : That because he conscientiously believes he is permitted by the law of God to labor on Sunday, he may violate with impunity the statute declaring it illegal to do so ; but a man's religious belief cannot be accepted as a justification for his committing an overt act made criminal by the law of the land. If the law operates harshly, as laws sometimes do, the remedy is in the hands of the legislature. It is not the province of the judiciary to pass upon the wisdom or policy of legislation. That is for the members of the legislative department ; and the only appeal from their determination is to the constituency."

This decision of the Supreme Court is of the same piece with the prosecutions and judicial processes throughout. It gives to the legislature all the omnipotence of the British Parliament, and in that does away with all necessity for a Constitution. The decision on this principle alone, is un-American. No legislative body in this country is framed upon the model of the British Parliament in respect to power. In this country, the powers of every legislature are defined and limited by Constitutions. It is the prerogative of Supreme Courts to define the meaning of the Constitution, and to decide whether an act of the legislature is Constitutional or not. If the act is Constitutional, then it must stand, whatever the results may be. And the Supreme Court is the body by which the Constitutionality or the unconstitutionality of any statute is to be discovered. But if, as this decision declares, the legislature is omnipotent, and that which it does must stand as law, then there is no use for a Constitution. "One of the objects for which the judiciary department is established, is the protection of the Constitutional rights of the citizens."

So long as there is a Constitution above the legislature, which defines and limits its powers, and protects and guards the rights of the citizens, so long it is the province of the Supreme Court to pronounce upon the acts of the legislature. The Supreme Court of Arkansas, therefore, in this case, clearly abdicated one of the very functions for which it was created, or else subverted the Constitution of Arkansas; and in either case, bestowed upon the legislature the omnipotence of the British Parliament, which is contrary to every principle of American institutions. Nor is the State of Arkansas an exception in this case; for this is the usual procedure of Supreme Courts in sustaining Sunday laws. They cannot be sustained upon any American principle; resort has to be made in every instance, and has been with scarcely an exception, either to the church-and-state principles of the British Government, or to the British principle of the omnipotence of the legislative power. But American principles are far above and far in advance of the principles of the British Government, in that they recognize Constitutional limitations upon the legislative power, and countenance no union of church and state; consequently Sunday laws never have been, and never can be, sustained upon American principles.

That this stricture upon the Supreme Court of Arkansas is not unjust, we have the clearest proof. The three judges who then composed the Supreme Court, were all members of the Bar Association of the State of Arkansas. In less than three months after this decision was rendered, the Bar Association *unanimously* made a report to the State on "law and law reform," an official copy of which I have in my possession. In that report, under the heading "Sunday Laws," is the following:—

"Our statute as it stands in Mansfield's Digest, provides that 'persons who are members of any religious

society who observe as Sabbath any other day of the
week than the Christian Sabbath, or Sunday, shall not
be subject to the penalties of this act [the Sunday law],
so that they observe one day in seven, agreeably to the
faith and practice of their church or society.' — *Mans.
Dig., sec. 1886.*

" This statute had been in force from the time of the
organization of the State government ; but it was un-
fortunately repealed by act of March 3, 1885. — *Acts
1885, p. 37.*

" While the Jews adhere, of course, to the letter of
the original command to remember the seventh day of
the week, there is also in the State a small but respect-
able body of Christians who consistently believe that
the seventh day is the proper day to be kept sacred ;
and in the case of Scoles *vs.* State, our Supreme Court
was compelled to affirm a judgment against a member
of one of these churches, for worshiping God according
to the dictates of his own conscience, supported, as he
supposed, by good theological arguments. It is very
evident that the system now in force, savoring, as it
does, very much of religious persecution, is a relic of
the Middle Ages, when it was thought that men could
be made orthodox by an act of parliament. Even in
Massachusetts, where Sabbatarian laws have always
been enforced with unusual vigor, exceptions are made
in favor of persons who religiously observe any other
day in the place of Sunday. We think that the law as
it stood in Mansfield's Digest, should be restored, with
such an amendment as would prevent the sale of spirits
on Sunday, as that was probably the object of repeal-
ing the above section."

Now the Arkansas Constitution says : —

" All men have a natural and indefeasible right to
worship Almighty God according to the dictates of their
own consciences ; no man can of right be compelled to
attend, erect, or support any place of worship, or to
maintain any ministry, against his consent. No human
authority can, in any case or manner whatsoever, control or interfere with the right of conscience ; and no

preference shall ever be given by law to any religious establishment, denomination, or mode of worship, above any other."

This report of the Bar Association says, "In the case of Scoles *vs.* State, our Supreme Court was compelled to affirm a judgment against a member of one of these churches, for worshiping God according to the dictates of his own conscience."

The members of the Supreme Court being members of the Bar Association, in that report it is confessed that they confirmed a judgment against a man for doing that which the Constitution explicitly declares all men have a natural and indefeasible right to do.

Senator Blair. — Then if they had a law like this, they were wrongly convicted under the law, just as innocent men are sometimes hung ; but you cannot reason that there should be no law against murder because innocent men are sometimes executed. It is a fault in the administration of the law. You cannot reason from that that there should be no law.

Mr. Jones. — If there had been arrests of other people for working on Sunday, in anything like the numbers that there were of seventh-day observers, and the law had been enforced upon all alike, then the iniquity would not have been so apparent ; or if those who were not seventh-day observers, and who were arrested, had been convicted, even then the case would not have been so clearly one of persecution. But when in all the record of the whole two years' existence of the law in this form, there was not a solitary saloon keeper arrested, there was not a person who did not observe the seventh day arrested, with the two exceptions named, then there could be no clearer demonstration that the law was used only as a means to vent religious spite against a class of citizens guiltless of any crime, but only of professing a religion different from that of the majority.

The fact of the matter is, — and the whole history of these proceedings proves it, — that from beginning to end these prosecutions were only the manifestation of that persecuting, intolerant spirit that will always make itself felt when any class of religionists can control the civil power. The information upon which the indictments were found, was treacherously given, and in the very spirit of the Inquisition. The indictment itself is a travesty of legal form, and a libel upon justice. The principle was more worthy of the Dark Ages than of any civilized nation or modern time ; and the Supreme Court decision that confirmed the convictions, is one which is contrary to the first principles of Constitutional law or Constitutional compacts.

And if Congress should lend its sanction to religious legislation to the extent of passing this national Sunday bill, now under consideration, and its principles should be made of force in all the States, the history of Arkansas from 1885–87 would be repeated through the whole extent of the nation. This I can prove, at least so far as the intention goes of those who are actively in favor of it. Rev. D. Mc Allister is one of the principal men of the National Reform Association. That Association and the Woman's Christian Temperance Union held a joint convention at Lakeside, Ohio, in July, 1887 ; and speaking on the subject of a national Sunday law, Dr. Mc Allister said : —

"Let a man be what he may, — Jew, seventh-day observer of some other denomination, or those who do not believe in the Christian Sabbath, — let the law apply to every one, that there shall be no public desecration of the first day of the week, the Christian Sabbath, the day of rest for the nation. They may hold any other day of the week as sacred, and observe it ; but that day which is the one day in seven for the nation at large, let that not be publicly desecrated by any one, by officer in the Government, or by private citizen, high or low, rich or poor."

Then some one stated from the audience that —

"There is a law in the State of Arkansas enforcing Sunday observance upon the people, and the result has been that many good persons have not only been imprisoned, but have lost their property, and even their lives."

To which Mr. Mc Allister coolly replied : —

"It is better that a few should suffer, than that the whole nation should lose its Sabbath."

This argument is identical with that by which the Pharisees in Christ's day justified themselves in killing him.   It was said : —

"It is expedient for us that one man should die for the people, and that the whole nation perish not." John 11 : 50.

And then says the record : —

"Then from that day forth they took counsel together for to put him to death."   Verse 53.

It is because of these principles, unblushingly avowed by the very men who stand in the lead in the effort to secure the enactment of this national Sunday law ; and because of the practical effect of such a law in Arkansas and Tennessee, and to some extent in Pennsylvania, — it is because of these things that we say to you, gentlemen of the United States Senate, you cannot afford to give to these men the power which they seek in the enactment of this proposed Sunday law.   The speech of Senator Crockett's, which I have read, was made in the legislature of Arkansas, when he was pleading for the restoration of that exemption clause, — when he was pleading for toleration, in fact.

Senator Blair. — Do you know whether this young man had money or friends ?

Mr. Jones. — Dr. Lewis, can you certify whether he had money?

Dr. Lewis. — The case was never reported to other churches for relief. I do not know as to his personal estate.

Senator Blair. — Do you not think it was a peculiar man who would allow his child to be killed and his wife to starve?

Dr. Lewis. — The case was not reported to our churches in the North.

Mr. Jones. — About that peculiarity I will say that John Bunyan stayed twelve years in Bedford jail when he could have got out by simply saying the word "yes," and agreeing that he would not preach.

Senator Blair. — It was a very different thing to be called on to say that he would abstain from the performance of a great duty in his church. He preached the gospel, and he would not agree not to preach the gospel. But here is a man who lets his wife and child die rather than pay twenty-five or fifty dollars and get out, and have an opportunity to go to work for them.

Mr. Jones. — What kind of law is that which puts a man upon his conscience to choose between his wife and child and paying a fine of twenty-five or fifty dollars? But suppose he had paid the fine, and got out and gone to work again, how long could he have worked? When the next Sunday came round, it was his duty to his wife and child to work for their support. Is he to go to work on Sunday, and go through the course of prosecution again, and again pay a fine of twenty-five or fifty dollars? How long could this be kept up? There are not many poor farmers who can clear from twenty-five to fifty dollars every week above all expenses, to be devoted to paying regular fines for the privilege of following their honest occupation on their own premises. But it will be said, " Let him not work on Sunday, then he would not have to pay a fine." Well, if he consents to do no work on Sunday, he consents to be robbed of one-sixth of his time, which he honestly owes to the support of his wife and child. For to rob him of one-sixth of his time is precisely what the State does in such a case ; and it is either confiscation outright, or confiscation under the guise of a fine imposed as punishment for his refusing to allow himself to be robbed of one-sixth of his time. Either this, or else he must give up his right to worship God according to the dictates of his own conscience and the word of God, and so surrender his rights of conscience altogether. It comes to this, therefore, that Sunday laws are a direct invasion of the rights of conscience.

More than this, Sunday laws are a direct invasion not only of the Constitutional right, but the inalienable right, of acquiring, possessing, and protecting property. I here adopt the language of the Supreme Court of California, — language which can never be successfully controverted : —

" The right to protect and possess property is not more clearly protected by the Constitution than the right to acquire. The right to acquire must include the right to use the proper means to attain the end. The right itself would be impotent without the power to use the necessary incidents. If the legislature have the authority to appoint a time of compulsory rest, . . . it is without limit, and may extend to the prohibition of all occupations at all times. . . . For the Constitution to declare a right inalienable and at the same time leave the legislature unlimited power over it, would be a contradiction in terms, an idle provision, proving that a Constitution was a mere parchment barrier, insufficient to protect the citizen, delusive and visionary, and the practical result of which would be to destroy, not conserve, the rights which they may assume to protect. The legislature, therefore, cannot prohibit the proper use of the means of acquiring property, except the peace and safety of the State require it."—*Ex parte Newman, 9 Cal., pp. 517, 510.*

But does the peace and safety of the State require it in any such case as is here involved? Can it ever be against the peace and safety of the State for any man to follow his honest, legitimate, and even laudable occupations? It is against the peace and safety of the State to *prohibit* it. For, as I have before conclusively proved, for the State to do so is for it to put honest occupations in the catalogue of crimes; to put peaceable and industrious citizens upon a level with criminals; and to put a premium upon idleness and recklessness. It is certainly against the peace and safety of any State to do any such thing. Therefore it is demonstrated that Sunday laws are an invasion of the inalienable right of acquiring and possessing property, and for that man in Arkansas to have obeyed that law, would have been to surrender his inalienable right.

Once more: As the right to acquire property includes the right to use the proper means to attain that end, and as such a law deprives a man of the use of such means during one-sixth of his time, it follows that it is a violation of that provision of the Fourteenth Amendment of the United States Constitution, which declares that " no State shall deprive any citizen of life, liberty, or property, without due process of law."

All this, sir, is involved in the question as to whether that man shall recognize the law to such an extent as even to pay the fine. If he does, then it follows inevitably that all his property shall go to pay fines, or else he must choose between yielding his rights of conscience, and allowing one-sixth of his time to be confiscated, and in that a certain proportion of property;

because to the industrious citizen, time is property. But if the State by a Sunday law or by any other means, may confiscate a part, it may confiscate all. Where, then, shall resistance to oppression begin ? — I say, At the very first appearance of it.   Under cover of the word "*loan*" Charles I. undertook to confiscate a small sum of money from each of the property owners of England.   John Hampden's share was about seven dollars and seventy-five cents.   He was a rich man, but he refused to pay it ; and his refusal to pay that paltry sum led to all England's being plunged into confusion and civil war : the king lost his head, Hampden himself lost his life, and all this rather than to pay the insignificant sum of seven dollars and seventy-five cents ! — less than one-third of the fine imposed upon this man for refusing to assent to the confiscation of one-sixth of his property.   But John Hampden's refusal to pay that money established the Constitutional principle that every man has the inalienable right to acquire, possess, and protect property — a right which was invaded in this case.   Upon this principle alone that man was entirely justified in refusing to pay the fine imposed by that Sunday law.   But as there was also involved the inalienable right of conscience, he was doubly justified in refusing to obey the law or to recognize the principle.

Senator Blair. — Suppose he was a guilty man. Suppose he did not believe it was an offense to steal, and that he conscientiously thought that he could take goods from another in a certain way.   He had been convicted under the law, and was under the penalty of paying twenty-five dollars' fine.   Is he to put his right of conscience against the demands of wife and child, and against the judgment of the community, and the State in which he lives, and to which he owes all the rights to the enjoyment of property, and everything

else he has ?   In this case a man saw all this evil done
rather than pay twenty-five or fifty dollars, and he says
he did that by reason of his conscience.

Mr. Jones. — The cases are not parallel at all, unless
indeed you count it as much of a crime for a man to
follow his honest occupation as it is for him to steal.
This, however, we have demonstrated is the very thing
that Sunday laws do.   But we forever protest against
honest industry's being put upon a level with thieving.

The man who steals takes the property of others
without compensation and without regard to the question of right.   If, then, the State takes from him property or time without compensation, he cannot complain
of injustice.   But in the case of the man who works on
Sunday, he invades no man's right in any degree ; he
takes no man's property or his time in any way, much
less does he take it without compensation.   For the
State to punish the thief, is just.   For the State to punish the industrious citizen, is pre-eminently unjust.

But aside from all this, did you ever hear of a man
whose conscience taught him that it was right to steal,
that it was a conscientious conviction to steal?

Senator Blair. — I have heard of a great many instances where an individual confessed that he had conscientiously violated the law, yet he was punished.

Mr. Jones. — Precisely ; and the Christians were put
to death under the Roman empire for violating the law.

Senator Blair. — But that does not answer my question, and it is not necessary that it should be answered.

Mr. Jones. — It is right for any man to violate any
law that invades his Constitutional rights ; and it is
his right conscientiously to violate any law that invades
the rights of conscience.   God declares the man innocent who violates the law that interferes with man's
relationship to God — the law that invades the rights of
conscience.   See cases "The King *vs.* Shadrach, Me-

shach, and Abed-nego ;" and "The State *vs.* Daniel," reported in Daniel, chapters 3 and 6.

The end of the Arkansas case, as reported by Senator Crockett, was that the poor man lost both his wife and his child.

Senator Blair. — What became of him ?

Mr. Jones. — He left the State.

Senator Blair. — I should think he ought to leave it.

Mr. Jones. — So do I, sir.   But what can be said of freedom any more in this country, when such things can be ?   That is also true of six other men who followed the dictates of their own consciences, — as good, honest, virtuous citizens as lived in Arkansas.

Senator Blair. — There is a good deal of humbug about the dictates of one's own conscience.   If a man is to set up his conscience against the obligations to do what is right and to perform his duty toward society, an unintelligent and uninformed conscience of that kind might be allowed to destroy all society.   It is not conscience always.

Mr. Jones. — I beg your pardon, sir.   The rights of conscience are eternally sacred.   There is no conscience in regard to the State, however ; conscience has to do with God, and with what he has commanded ; and a man reads in the Bible what God commands.   I here adopt the words of the present Associate-Justice of the Supreme Court of the United States, Hon. Stanley Matthews, in his speech in the case of the Cincinnati School Board *vs.* Minor *et al.*   He says : —

"We may call the eccentricities of conscience, vagaries, if we please ; but in matters of religious concern we have no right to disregard or despise them, no matter how trivial and absurd we may conceive them to be. In the days of the early Christian martyrs, the Roman lictors and soldiers despised and ridiculed the fanaticism that refused the trifling conformity of a pinch of incense upon the altar, erected to the Cæsar that arrogated to himself the title and honor of 'divine,' or of a heathen statue.   History is filled with the record of bloody sacrifices which holy men who feared God rather than men, have not withheld, on account of what seemed to cruel persecutors but trifling observances and concessions. . . . Conscience, if your honors please, is a tender thing, and tenderly to be regarded ; and in the same proportion in which a man treasures his own moral integrity, —sets up the light of conscience within him as the glory of God shining in him to discover to him the truth,— so ought he to regard the conscience of every other man, and apply the cardinal maxim of Christian life and practice, 'Whatsoever ye would that men should do to you, do ye even so unto them.'"

Senator Blair. — Should those who conscientiously believe in free love be allowed to indulge in it ?

Mr. Jones. — There is no point in that.   Where is there any conscientious conviction in free love ?   I cannot discover it.   There is no room for any.

Senator Blair. — But there must be laws which prohibit immorality ?

Mr. Jones. — I ask you to define what immorality is, and then I will answer your question.

Senator Blair. — If you do not know what the expression means, I shall not undertake to enlighten you.

Mr. Jones. — I know what it means.

Senator Blair. — Then why do you ask me to define it ?   Why do you not answer the question ?

Mr. Jones. — Because there are modified meanings of the word which make it refer to crime.   Immorality is itself a violation of the law of God, and civil government has no right to punish any man for a violation of the law of God as such.   I do say, therefore, that that which, properly speaking, is immorality, the civil law cannot prohibit, and that it has no right to attempt it.   Morality is defined as follows ; —

"*Morality:* The relation of conformity or non-conformity to the true moral standard or rule. . . . The conformity of an act to the divine law."

As morality is the conformity of an act to the divine law, it is plain that morality pertains solely to God, and with that, civil government can have nothing to do.

Again: Moral law is defined as —

"The will of God, as the supreme moral ruler, concerning the character and conduct of all responsible beings; the rule of action as obligatory on the conscience or moral nature." "The moral law is summarily contained in the decalogue, written by the finger of God on two tables of stone, and delivered to Moses on Mount Sinai."

These definitions are evidently according to Scripture. The Scriptures show that the ten commandments are the law of God; that they express the will of God; that they pertain to the conscience, and take cognizance of the thoughts and intents of the heart; and that obedience to these commandments is the duty that man owes to God. Says the Scripture, —

"Fear God, and keep his commandments; for this is the whole duty of man." Eccl. 12 : 13.

And the Saviour says, –

"Ye have heard that it was said by them of old time, Thou shalt not kill; and whosoever shall kill shall be in danger of the judgment; but I say unto you that whosoever is angry with his brother without a cause, shall be in danger of the judgment; and whosoever shall say to his brother, Raca [vain fellow, *margin*], shall be in danger of the council; but whosoever shall say, Thou fool, shall be in danger of hell fire." Matt. 5 : 21, 22.

The apostle John, referring to the same thing, says, —

"Whosoever hateth his brother is a murderer." 1 John 3 : 15.

Again, the Saviour says, —

"Ye have heard that it was said by them of old time, Thou shalt not commit adultery; but I say unto you that whosoever looketh on a woman to lust after her, hath committed adultery with her already in his heart." Matt. 5 : 27, 28.

Other illustrations might be given, but these are sufficient to show that obedience to the moral law is morality; that it pertains to the thoughts and intents of the heart, and therefore, in the very nature of the case, lies beyond the reach or control of the civil power. To hate is murder; to covet is idolatry; to think impurely of a woman is adultery; — these are all equally immoral, and violations of the moral law, but no civil government seeks to punish for them. A man may hate his neighbor all his life; he may covet everything on earth; he may think impurely of every woman that he sees, — he may keep it up all his days; but so long as these things are confined to his thought, the civil power cannot touch him. It would be difficult to conceive of a more immoral person than such a man would be; yet the State cannot punish him. It does not attempt to punish him. This demonstrates again that with morality or immorality the State can have nothing to do.

But let us carry this further. Only let that man's hatred lead him, either by word or sign, to attempt an injury to his neighbor, and the State will punish him; only let his covetousness lead him to lay hands on what is not his own, in an attempt to steal, and the State will punish him; only let his impure thought lead him to attempt violence to any woman, and the State will punish him. Yet bear in mind that even then the State does not punish him for his immorality, but for his *incivility*. The immorality lies in the heart, and can be measured by God only. The State punishes no man because he is immoral. If it did, it would have to punish as a mur-

derer the man who hates another, and to punish as an
idolater the man who covets, and to punish as an adul-
terer the one who thinks impurely ; because according
to the true standard of morality, hatred is murder, covetousness is idolatry, and impurity of thought is adultery. Therefore it is clear that in fact the State punishes no man because he is immoral, but because he is
uncivil. It cannot punish immorality ; it must punish
incivility.

This distinction is shown in the very term by which
is designated State or national government ; it is called
civil government. No person but a theocrat ever thinks
of calling it moral government. The government of
God is the only moral government. God is the only
moral governor. The law of God is the only moral law.
To God alone pertains the punishment of immorality,
which is the transgression of the moral law. Governments of men are civil governments, not moral. The
laws of States and nations are civil laws, not moral. To
the authorities of civil government pertains the punishment of incivility, that is, the transgression of civil law.
It is not theirs to punish immorality. That pertains
solely to the Author of the moral law and of the moral
sense, who is the sole judge of man's moral relation. All
this must be manifest to every one who will think fairly
upon the subject, and it is confirmed by the definition of
the word *civil*, which is this : —

"*Civil:* Pertaining to a city or State, or to a citizen
in his relations to his fellow-citizens, or to the State."

Thus it is made clear that we owe to Cæsar (civil
government) only that which is civil, and that we owe
to God that which is moral or religious, and that to no
man, to no assembly or organization of men, does there
belong any right whatever to punish immorality. Whoever attempts it, usurps the prerogative of God. The

Inquisition is the inevitable logic of any claim of any assembly of men to punish immorality ; because to punish immorality, it is necessary in some way to get at the thoughts and intents of the heart.   The papacy, asserting the right to compel men to be moral, and to punish them for immorality, had the cruel courage to carry the evil principle to its logical consequence.   In carrying out the principle, it was found to be essential to get at the secrets of men's hearts ; and it was found that the diligent application of torture would wring from men, in many cases, a full confession of the most secret counsels of their hearts.   Hence the Inquisition was established as the means best adapted to secure the desired end.   So long as men grant the proposition that it is within the province of civil government to enforce morality, it is to very little purpose that they condemn the Inquisition ; for that tribunal is only the logical result of the proposition.

Thus much on the subject of morality and the State in the true and genuine sense of the word *morality.*   But as I said at the beginning, there is an accommodated sense in which the word *morality* is used, in which it is made to refer only to men's relations to their fellowmen ; and with reference to this view of morality, it is sometimes said that the civil power is to enforce morality *upon a civil basis.*   But morality on a civil basis is only civility, and the enforcement of morality upon a civil basis is the enforcement of civility, and nothing else.   Without the Inquisition, it is impossible for civil government ever to carry its jurisdiction beyond civil things, or to enforce anything but civility.

But it may be asked, Does not the civil power enforce the observance of the commandments of God, which say, "Thou shalt not steal," "Thou shalt not kill," "Thou shalt not commit adultery," and "Thou shalt not bear false witness"?   Does not the civil power punish the violation of these commandments of God? I answer: The civil power does not enforce these, nor does it punish the violation of them, *as commandments of God.* The State does forbid murder and theft and perjury, and some States forbid adultery, but not as commandments of God. From time immemorial, governments that knew nothing about God, have forbidden these things. If the State is to enforce these things as the commandments of God, it will have to take cognizance of the thoughts and intents of the heart ; but this is not within the province of any earthly power.

By all these evidences is established the plain, common-sense principle that to civil government pertains only that which the term itself implies, — that which is civil. The purpose of civil government is civil, and not moral. Its function is to preserve order in society, and to cause all its subjects to rest·in assured safety, by guarding ·them against all incivility. Morality belongs to God ; civility, to the State. Morality must be rendered to God ; civility, to the State. Immorality must be punished — *can* be punished — only by the Lord. Incivility must be punished — and no more than that *can* possibly be punished — by the State.

Here, then, at the close of my remarks, we are brought to the enunciation of the eternal principle with which I began, upon which we now stand, and upon which we forever expect to stand, — the principle embodied in the United States Constitution forbidding religious tests, and forbidding Congress to make any law respecting an establishment of religion or prohibiting the free exercise thereof, — the principle established by Jesus Christ : *Render therefore* UNTO CÆSAR *the things which are* CÆSAR'S ; *and* UNTO GOD THE THINGS THAT ARE GOD'S.

REMARKS BY REV. A. H. LEWIS, D. D.

Dr. Lewis. — Mr. Chairman. The objection raised by Prof. Jones against the exemption in favor of Sabbath-keepers, seems to me wholly imaginary. So far as any Seventh-day Baptists are concerned, I know it would be impossible for any man opening a saloon on Sunday to present the excuse that he was a Seventh-day Baptist. A saloon-keeping Seventh-day Baptist is an unknown thing throughout their history of more than two centuries. Such a man could not obtain recognition, much less church membership, in any Seventh-day Baptist community or church. Nor do I believe from what I know of the Seventh-day Adventists, that such a case could occur in connection with that people. The possibility of any such deceitful claim could easily be guarded against by a provision requiring that in any case of doubt the one claiming to have observed the seventh day should be required to bring official certificate of his relation to a Sabbath-keeping church. Such a provision would end all difficulty.

REPLY.

Mr. Jones. — Mr. Chairman. It is certainly true that, so far, a saloon-keeping Seventh-day Baptist, or Seventh-day Adventist, either, is an unknown thing. But if Sunday laws are enforced with an exemption clause in favor of those who keep the seventh day, this would not be an unknown thing much longer. It is true, also, that such a man could not obtain membership in any Seventh-day Baptist or Seventh-day Adventist church. But what is to prevent the saloon keepers from organizing Seventh-day Baptist or Seventh-day Adventist churches of their own, and for themselves? What is to prevent them, or any class of business men, from organizing their own churches, electing their own officers, and even ordaining their own pastors, and calling them-

selves Seventh-day Baptists or Seventh-day Adventists?
There is nothing to prevent it ; unless, indeed, the State
itself shall take charge of all seventh-day churches and
doctrines, and attend to their organization and the ad-
mission of members. This is precisely what was done
before. In the days of the New England theocracy,
Massachusetts enacted a law that,—

"For the time to come, no man shall be admitted to
the freedom of this body politic, but such as are members of some of the churches within the limits of the
same."

There were considerable numbers of men who were
not members of any of the churches, and who could
not be, because they were not Christians. These men
then took to forming themselves into churches of their
own. Then the next step for the authorities to take,
and they took it, was to enact a law that,—

"Forasmuch as it hath bene found by sad experience
that much trouble and disturbance hath happened both
to the church and civill State by the officers and members of some churches, wch have bene gathered . . .
in an undue manner, . . . it is . . . ordered that . . .
this Court doeth not, nor will hereafter, approue of any
such companyes of men as shall henceforthe ioyne in
any pretended way of church fellowshipp, without
they shall first acquainte the magistrates and elders of
the greatr pte of the churches in this jurisdicon, with
their intencons, and have their approbacon herein."—
Emancipation of Massachusetts, pp. 28-30.

By this, gentlemen, you will see that the enactment
of this Sunday law, though the first step, will not be by
any means the last step, and that in more directions
than one. Their offer of an exemption clause is a
voluntary confession that the enforcement of the law
without one would be unjust ; but if that exemption
clause be embodied and maintained, the State is

inevitably carried beyond its proper jurisdiction; and if the exemption clause is retained and not maintained in its strictness, the whole law is at once nullified. Congress would better learn wisdom from this prospect, and utterly refuse to have anything at all to do with the subject. The whole subject is beyond the jurisdiction of the civil power, and the civil power can do no better than to let it entirely alone.

But Dr. Lewis proposes to guard against all difficulty, by "requiring" every observer of the seventh day "to bring official certificate of his relation to a Sabbath-keeping church." This would not end the difficulty; for, as I have shown, it would inevitably devolve upon the State to decide what was a genuine Sabbath-keeping church. But that is not the worst feature in this suggestion. If Dr. Lewis officially represents the Seventh-day Baptist denomination, and for the denomination proposes thus voluntarily to put himself and all his people on "ticket of leave," I have no particular objection; that is their own business; yet it seems to me an extremely generous proposition, if not an extraordinary proceeding. I say *they* may do this, if they choose. But as for me and for the Seventh-day Adventists generally, not only as Christians, but as American citizens, we repudiate with scorn and reject with utter contempt every principle of any such suggestion. As citizens of the United States, and as Christians, we utterly and forever refuse to put ourselves upon "ticket of leave" by any such proposition.

———

NOTE. — That my argument at first was not so unfounded nor so "wholly imaginary" as Dr. Lewis supposed, has been conclusively demonstrated, even to himself, since this hearing was held. The "Pearl of

Days" column of the New York *Mail and Express*, the official organ of the American Sunday Union, in March, 1889, gave the following statement from the Plainfield [N. J.] *Times* [no date] : —

"As a rule, Plainfield, N. J., is a very quiet city on Sunday. Liquor, provision, and cigar stores are closed by the enforcement of a city ordinance. If a resident wants a cigar, he will either have it given to him by one of the many pharmacists who refuse to sell on Sunday, or he will go to the two dealers who are allowed to open their places on Sunday because they observe Saturday as their Sabbath. Some time ago a man of Catholic faith, who had an eye to Sunday business in that line, became a regular attendant at the Seventh-day Baptist church. Eventually he asked to be admitted into the fellowship of the church. A member of the official board was advised that the applicant for membership was only working for business ends. He was closely examined by the church officers, and he finally admitted that he wanted to open a cigar store and do business on Sunday. The man appeared at the wrong place for aid in carrying out his mercenary purposes. He was not received into membership."

It looks somewhat like the " irony of fate " that this thing should fall to the very people whom Dr. Lewis represented, and in the very town where Dr. Lewis himself lives.

REMARKS BY MRS. J. C. BATEHAM.

Mrs. Batcham. — I should like to say that the point which has been made was a point carefully considered by the Woman's Christian Temperance Union, and we saw the danger. Yet we wished to be exceedingly fair. I consulted nine persons of different classes of Seventh-day people, to know whether they wished such an exemption, and whether they would be satisfied with what was proposed. They represented themselves as being in approval of some such provision as has been suggested, and we thought it could be done perhaps in such a way as to afford them the exemption which they desire, because they said that such an exemption is necessary.

Senator Blair. — Let me ask you a few questions, Mrs. Batcham, to see if the Woman's Christian Temperance Union understood exactly the relation of what they propose to do in this legislation. Here is a bill which relates to interstate commerce, to postal work, to the army, and to the navy. It relates to that subject-matter which is carved out of the independent, full jurisdiction of a nation by the States, which were once complete sovereignties, and transferred to the general Government. The occupations I have mentioned are all of public nature ; and to carry them on, the nation has such an opportunity to invade the Sabbath-rest laws of every State in such a way as to nullify them. The nation at large is unrestrained by any Sabbath law whatever. If it may carry on its post-office business on the Sabbath, it may go to any extent, and it does go already to a very great extent, and an increasingly great extent ; so in regard to interstate commerce, and so with the army and the navy.

Now, you go to our Seventh-day Baptist or Seventh-day Adventist friends, for instance, and propose to introduce a principle by which they can carry on the post-office department on the Sabbath, just as completely as they see fit. In other words, you propose to exempt them from the operation of the law so far as it prohibits post-office work on the Sabbath. Suppose you have a Seventh-day Baptist man for postmaster. Suppose you fill up every post-office in the country on the Sabbath with Seventh-day Baptist people. You have the post-office department in operation by virtue of this exemption, because they can do the work conscientiously on that day. If you limit it by saying the bill shall not apply to the Adventists and others, the bill provides that already.

Mrs. Bateham. — If you remember the clause, we do not propose to provide that they shall be able to do this work, but that they shall be exempt from the penalty. They are not allowed to do the work, but they are to be exempt from the penalty. Therefore, unless they could prove that they had not done the work to the disturbance of others, it would be impossible for them to carry on post-office matters, for instance, or any other public employment, on Sunday.

Senator Blair. — Is not that equivalent to saying that if the penalty shall not be enforced against them, there shall be no law against them ? Because the law without the penalty is simply an opinion ; it is not a law.

Mrs. Bateham. — The law could provide that they should not open a post-office, for instance, or any place of business ; and if there was a fine imposed, they would be compelled to close such places on Sunday. It was, of course, only thrown out as a suggestion from us that if it could be done, we should like to have such a provision in the bill. We are satisfied that people want the law, and if the law can, in your wisdom, be arranged with such an exemption, then we wish it ; otherwise we do not. We are all glad, I think, to have the gentlemen admit that they do not want such an exemption, for that releases us from the place where we were.

Senator Blair. — This is not to be a general Sunday law. These people all live in States, and they can work at their private occupations just the same under similar amendments to the State law, if the State saw fit to make such amendments. Prof. Jones says it did not work well in Arkansas, and I should think it did not, from his description. But these are public occupations, or *quasi* public occupations, we are dealing with ; that of interstate commerce, for instance, carried on by great corporations which are public in their relation to the working-men, because they are exercising a great public function in carrying on transportation which appertains to everybody all over the country.

This proposed law undertakes to prohibit the nullification of all Sunday-rest laws in the States so far as to provide that interstate commerce shall not be carried on, in violation of the law, upon. the Sabbath. When you come to the private occupations which are regulated by the States, if they choose to allow the Seventh-day Baptist people to work on Sunday in those private occupations, on the farm, in the workshop, in the factory, this measure does not interfere with them at all.

Mrs. Bateham. — I have not the words before me, but my impression is that there is a clause in the bill providing that the jurisdiction of Congress shall be exercised over the Territories in. this matter. There is something of that kind in the bill, and this proposed exemption was designed to reach those cases, rather than apply to the general governmental action.

Senator Blair. — You think the exemption might be made with reference to the Territories?

Mrs. Bateham. — Yes; that was the point we had in mind in this general action. I have not the words of the bill before me, but there is something of that kind in it which we had in mind. I wish to say also that one of the requests of our National Woman's Christian Union was that the word *promote* should be changed to *protect*, in the title of the bill, so that it should have no appearance of what all Americans object to, any union of church and state. That amendment was proposed and accepted by the American Sabbath Union, the organized body which has just been in session in this city.

Senator Blair. — Do you not think that the word *protect* implies power to command and compel? An army protects.

Mrs. Bateham. — All our laws protect us, do they not?

Senator Blair. — You would make this a law?

Mrs. Bateham. — I suggest that the bill be made a law, and that it be a law which shall protect the civil Sabbath, not promote religious worship, but protect the day as a day of rest and religious worship.

Senator Blair. — It seems to me that the word *protect* is a stronger and more interfering word than *promote*. However, all these suggestions are important

REPLY.

Mr. Jones. — Mr. Chairman. Mrs. Bateham in her first address this morning, in telling who they are that are in favor of this Sunday law, said that she believed "the great majority of the people will approve such a law." She mentioned as opposed to it only "the daily newspaper press," "the railroad managers," "steamboat companies," "saloonists and their backers," "a class of foreigners who prefer the continental Sunday," and "the very small sect of Seventh-day Baptists."

Hon. G. P. Lord in his remarks said that "not more than three million of our population work on Sabbath, and most of this number are unwilling workers." He said that "the balance, or more than fifty-seven million of our population, abstain from toil on the Sabbath."

Taking these statements as the truth, it appears that the overwhelming majority of the American people are not only in favor of the Sunday law, but they actually keep that day as a rest day.

Now, gentlemen, is it not rather singular, and a doctrine altogether new in a government of the people, that the *majority* need to be *protected?* From whom are they to be protected? — From themselves, most assuredly, because by their own representation they are so vastly in the majority that it would be impossible for them to be oppressed by anybody else. But in a government of the people, when the majority are oppressing themselves, how can laws prevent it when the laws must be made by the majority, that is, by the very ones who are carrying on the oppression? If to them my argument seems unsound, I would cite, entirely for their benefit, the words of the Supreme Court of Ohio, that the "protection" guaranteed in our Constitutional provisions "means protection to the minority. The majority can protect itself. Constitutions are enacted for the purpose of protecting the weak against the strong, the few against the many."

This is sound sense, as well as sound Constitutional law. Now, suppose in accordance with this sound Constitutional principle, and under cover of their own statements, we, seventh-day observers, whom they themselves designate as being so entirely in the minority as scarcely to be worthy of recognition, — suppose we should come to Congress asking for protection (and as all my argument has shown, if anybody needs protection in this matter, assuredly it is ourselves), — suppose, then, we come to Congress asking for protection in the same way that *they* ask for it, — suppose we should ask Congress to enact a law compelling all people to do no work on Saturday, in order to protect us in our right to keep Saturday ; what would be thought of that? what would these people themselves think of it? what ought anybody to think of it, but that it was a piece of unwarranted assumption of authority to force upon others our ideas of religious observances? That is all it would be, and it would be utterly inexcusable. And I risk nothing in saying that these people themselves, as well as everybody else, would pronounce it unwarrantable and inexcusable. But if that would be so in the case of a minority who actually need to be protected, what, then, ought *not* to be thought of these people who claim to be in the overwhelming majority, in their mission here, asking Congress to compel everybody to rest on Sunday for *their* protection !

Gentlemen, it is not protection, but *power*, that they want.

REMARKS BY JOHN B. WOOD.

Mr. Wood.—Mr. Chairman. As a member of the society of Friends, a Quaker, I should like to say a few words.

I have a great deal of sympathy with people who talk about the right of conscience. I do not think the United States Government has any right over the conscience. We, as Friends, deny their right over our consciences while we act in accordance with the revealed will of God, the Bible.

In looking at this Sunday question, I see nothing in the Bible — there is no word in it — in which it is stated that we shall have to work on the first day of the week. Therefore, I do not think the Seventh-day Baptists have any right to object to the proposed legislation. The only thing they lose is one more day's work out of the week.

The society of Friends has always denied the right to fight. The result has been that in the United States they have never lost a life by that means, not even during the last war. The Lord Jesus Christ has always protected them.

I think that any Saturday Baptist who believes honestly that the Sabbath is Saturday, can depend upon the Lord's providing for him in five days of the week just as well as if he worked six, and he will have two Sundays instead of one, and be that much better off.

REPLY.

Mr. Jones. — In answer to the question raised by Mr. Wood, that conscientious convictions do not require us to work on the first day of the week, one of the six working days, I wish to say, —

First, we deny his right, as well as the right of the State, to assume the prerogative of deciding for us what the Bible teaches, or what our conscientious convictions do, or do not, require.

Secondly, we deny the right of the State to cause us to lose the whole, or any part, of a day's work out of every week. And I turn this point upon him as I turned it upon the others, Why have we not as much right to ask for a law compelling them to rest on the day that we keep, as they have to compel us to rest on the day which they keep? "The only thing they would lose is one more day's work out of the week." Then they could "have two Sundays instead of one, and be that much better off." Why is it not as good for them as it is for us? Or is this a benefit reserved solely for those who do *not* keep Sunday? How this invades the Constitutional right of acquiring and possessing property, and does deprive us of property without due process of law, I have already discussed.

Thirdly, upon this point I wish to read Judge Cooley's opinion.

Mr. Wood. — I referred to the Bible.

Mr. Jones. — The Bible says, "Six days shalt thou labor." While I do not insist that this is an absolute command that we shall actually work the whole six days, I do insist that it is a God-given permission, and therefore our God-given right, to work six days of every week. And we deny forever the right of the State to forbid us to do that which, to say the very least, God has given us the express right to do.

As this is a matter of legislation and therefore of law, Judge Cooley's opinion is of weight upon the subject. He says : —

"The Jew [and the seventh-day Christian as well] who is forced to respect the first day of the week, when his conscience requires of him the observance of the seventh also, may plausibly urge that the law discriminates against his religion, and by forcing him to keep a second Sabbath in each week, *unjustly*, though by indirection, *punishes him for his belief.*"

I have shown —

Senator Blair. — He says "plausibly." That word *plausibly* indicates that there are some counter views somewhere.

Mr. Jones. — As to the exact sense in which he uses the word *plausibly*, of course we cannot tell without consulting Mr. Cooley himself; but I do not see why we should put the strongest meaning into the word, especially as farther on he shows that the argument of the Seventh-day keeper is unanswerable. I am inclined to think that the Judge uses the word there in the sense of fairly, rightly, or feasibly.

Next he says : —

"The laws which prohibit ordinary employments on Sunday are to be defended, either on the same grounds which justify the punishment of profanity, or as establishing sanitary regulations based upon the demonstration of experience that one day's rest in seven is needful to recuperate the exhausted energies of body and mind."

That is one of the pretended grounds of this petition for this national Sunday law ; but the answer of the Supreme Court of California to that is this : —

"This argument is founded on the assumption that mankind are in the habit of working too much, and thereby entailing evil upon society ; and that, without compulsion, they will not seek the necessary repose which their exhausted natures demand. This is to us a new theory, and is contradicted by the history of the past and the observations of the present. We have heard in all ages of declamations and reproaches against the vice of indolence ; but we have yet to learn that there has ever been any general complaint of an intemperate, vicious, unhealthy, or morbid industry. On the contrary, we know that mankind seek cessation from toil, from the natural influences of self-preservation, in the same manner and as certainly as they seek slumber, relief from pain, or food to appease their hunger. . . . If we cannot trust free agents to regulate their own labor, its times and quantity, it is difficult to trust them to make their own contracts. If the legislature could prescribe the days of rest for them, then it would seem that the same power could prescribe the hours to work, rest, and eat."—*Ex parte Newman, 9 Cal. 509, 518.*

And Judge Cooley's answer to it is this : —

" The Supreme Court of Pennsylvania have preferred to defend such legislation on the second ground rather than the first, but it appears to us that if the benefit of the individual is alone to be considered, the argument against the law which he may make who has already observed the seventh day of the week, is unanswerable."

Senator Blair. — But he also holds that for the general, the public good, Sunday laws are Constitutional.

Mr. Jones. — Yes ; and to be sustained upon authority. For the next sentence says : —

"But on the other ground, it is clear that these laws are supportable on authority, notwithstanding the inconvenience which they occasion to those whose religious sentiments do not recognize the sacred character of the first day of the week."

It is something unusual for persons to undertake to answer an unanswerable argument. But Judge Cooley employs here the only means by which an unanswerable argument can ever be answered: and that is, "on authority." That is the way the papacy has done it from the days of Pope Zosimus, A. D., 418, who, when asked for the reasons for certain of his arrogant actions, exclaimed: "So it has pleased the Apostolic See!" That was a sufficient answer to all inquiries, and even to unanswerable arguments.

England fastened upon the American colonies the Stamp Act. Our fathers presented unanswerable arguments against it; but the Stamp Act, like Judge Cooley's Constitutional Sunday laws, was supportable "on authority," and that was enough. England proposed to enforce it. But our revolutionary fathers refused assent to any such method of answering unanswerable arguments. So we refuse our assent to Mr. Cooley's answer to that which he himself pronounces an unanswerable argument.

Senator Blair. — It does not follow that there is no unanswerable argument in support of Sunday laws, I take it.

Mr. Jones. — There is the authority.

Senator Blair. — There is authority for the Sunday laws. It does not follow because the Sunday laws are supported by authority that therefore there is no sufficient argument upon which to base them.

Mr. Jones. — What authority is there for Sunday laws?

Senator Blair. — That is what you have been discussing; but you seem to say that because Sunday laws are supported "by authority," it is the only argument in favor of a bad law that there is authority for it. But there may be good authority for the Sunday law.

Mr. Jones. — That is what is shown here, that there is no good authority for it when it unjustly punishes a man for his belief. There cannot be any good authority

for unjustly punishing any man for anything, much less
for unjustly punishing him for his belief.

Senator Blair. — He does not say it is bad.

Mr. Jones. — But it *is* bad. Is there any good
answer to an unanswerable argument ?

Now, I propose to find out what authority there is
for Sunday laws.

I before referred to the decision of the Supreme Court
of Arkansas, and have shown from a statement of the
committee on "law and law reform," of which the
members of the Supreme Court were members, that
that decision was unconstitutional. I have shown that
the principle upon which their decision rested was that
of the omnipotence of parliament. In this, however,
the State of Arkansas only followed the decisions of
other States. In 1858, the Constitution of California
said, in Section 4 : " The free exercise and enjoyment
of religious profession and worship without discrimination or preference shall forever be allowed in this
State." There was a statute passed by the legislature
enforcing the observance of " the Christian Sabbath," on
the first day of the week. A Jew in Sacramento kept
his store open on Sunday ; he was arrested, convicted,
and sent to jail. He sued out a writ of *habeas corpus*
on the ground of " the illegality of his imprisonment
by reason of the unconstitutionality of the law." The
majority of the court sustained the plea by decisions
separately written, whose soundness, both upon Constitutional principles and upon the abstract principle of
justice itself, can never be successfully controverted.
Mr. Stephen J. Field, now Associate-Justice of the Supreme Court of the United States, was then a member
of the California Court. He rendered a dissenting
opinion, taking the same position as the Supreme
Court of Arkansas as to the omnipotence of the legislature, and soberly maintaining that the term " Chris-

tian Sabbath" in the act was not a discrimination or preference in favor of any religious profession or worship. He declared that "moralists and statesmen," "men of science and distinguished philosophers," have pronounced the rule of "one day's rest in seven" to be "founded upon a law of our race." But he omitted to state what scientist or philosopher or moralist or statesman has ever pronounced upon what law is founded the rule of *two* days' rest in seven for the man who chooses to rest some other day than Sunday!

In his written opinion, Mr. Field said that he had found that in twenty-five States of the Union, Sunday laws had been held to be Constitutional.. That this is so there can be no doubt. On this subject, as on that of blasphemy, which I have already noticed, the younger States, both in legislation and judicial decisions, have followed the example of the older States; these have followed the decisions of the oldest, and the oldest followed the example and the precedents of the colonies; and every one of the colonies had Sunday laws because every one had an established religion. These followed the precedents of the English system, which is wholly a church-and-state system. The church-and-state system of England severed itself from the papal rule when Henry VIII. renounced allegiance to the pope, and put himself at the head of the church of England in the place of the pope. The British system at that time was the papal system; the papal system was established by the mutual craft, flattery, and policy of Constantine and the ambitious bishops of his time, when the first Sunday law was enacted. This, in a word, is the genealogy of the Sunday laws of the United States. They belong with an established religion, — a union of church and state. And in this country they have been almost universally sustained, either upon the British principle of the omnipotence of parliament, or upon the church and state principles of the colonies, of the British government, and of the papacy.

The law of Pennsylvania, sustained by the decision referred to by Judge Cooley, was virtually a colonial law, which was a part of the system in which nobody who did "not confess and acknowledge one Almighty God to be the Creator, upholder, and ruler of the world," could be a citizen.

The Supreme Court of New York sustains Sunday laws by at once declaring Christianity to be the established religion of that State. This is based upon Chief Justice Kent's decision before referred to, which cited a law of the colony which declared that "the profanation of the Lord's day was 'the great scandal of the Christian faith.'" That decision of Judge Kent's made Christianity the established religion of the State of New York, by citing the precedents of the papal institutions of modern Europe and the pagan nations of antiquity.

This, again, proves Sunday laws to belong with established religions, with the union of church and state, finding their basis in papal and pagan institutions.

In every statute book in America, with scarcely an exception, Sunday laws are found under the head of "offenses against religion," or "offenses against God and religion." This springs naturally from the colonial legislation, where each colony deemed itself the special guardian of God and of some particular form of religion.

But according to the word of Christ, the civil power has nothing to do with either God or religion, nor with offenses against God or religion. Religion is defined by Webster as "the recognition of God as an object of worship, love, and obedience." Another definition, given by the National Reform Association itself, is "man's personal relation of faith and obedience to God." Civil government has nothing to do with a man's per-

sonal relation of faith and obedience to God.   If he has
no faith at all, and makes no pretensions to obedience to
God, that is nothing to the civil government, so long as
the man conducts himself civilly.   Neither has civil
government anything to do with offenses against God ;
the Lord himself can attend to that.   A man is responsible alone to God for the offenses which he commits
against God.   Civil government has no business to
establish a religion, and then make offenses against it
criminal ; nor has it any business to put itself in the
place of God, and presume to declare that an offense
against *the governmental idea of God* is an offense
against God.   How is the civil government to know
whether an act offends God or not ?   The fact of the
matter is, that just as soon as Sunday laws are investigated at all in the light of truth, or justice, or law,
it is found that they are inseparable from an established religion, — inseparable from a union of church
and state.

This is further shown by a mere glance at the British
system, as set forth by Blackstone in his chapter on
"Offenses against God and religion."   There "profanation of the Lord's day" is classed with such things
as "apostasy," "heresy," "reviling the ordinances of
the church," "non-comformity to the worship of the
church," "witchcraft," "conjuration," "enchantment,"
"sorcery," "religious imposture, such as falsely pre-
tending an extraordinary commission from heaven,"
adultery as an ecclesiastical offense cognizable by the
spiritual court, and such confusion of civil and religious ideas as the punishment of drunkenness as an offense against God and religion.   This is the company
with which Sunday laws belong.   The penalty for
apostasy was, first, burning to death ; this fell into
disuse after a while.   Then the penalty was that "for

the first offense the offender should be rendered incapable to hold any office or place of trust."

At such legal nonsense as this the United States Constitution struck a death blow in the clause which declares that "no religious test shall ever be required as a qualification to any office or public trust under this Government." And by the first amendment to the Constitution of the United States, this Government utterly separated itself from the whole system of offenses against God and religion so long maintained by the British government, by the colonies, and even yet by many of the States, and which is characteristic of all church-and-state governments — governments of established religion — by declaring that "Congress shall make no law respecting an establishment of religion, or prohibiting the free exercise thereof." This is sound American principle, and accords with the word of Jesus Christ. And the effort ought to be, throughout this whole nation, to lift the constitutions, the legislation, and the jurisprudence of the States up to the level of that of the national Constitution. But instead of doing that, and so carrying this whole nation bodily onward in the march of liberty, enlightenment, and progress, these people go about to bring down our national system of Constitution and laws to the level of that of the States, which is the level of that of the colonies, which is the level of that of the British system, which is the level of that of the papacy, which is the system of paganism under cover of the Christian name.

Dr. Elliott here to-day cited Edgar, Athelstan, and Alfred in support of Sunday laws. To be sure! And with equal force he can cite these and many others of the Dark Ages in support of tithes to the clergy, the supremacy of the monks in civil affairs, the "holy anointing" of kings by the pope, and for any and every

other thing that belongs with the papal system. He
can carry his Sunday-law precedents farther back than
that : he can go back to the time of Theodosius and Constantine.   He can find, and so can you or anybody else,
that as *Pontifex Maximus* of the old pagan system, Constantine "had the plenary power of appointing holy
days ;" he can find that by virtue of this power, Constantine established the first Sunday-law of all time, in
honor of the "venerable day of the sun," whose special
devotee he was ; and also that, as "bishop of exter-
nals" of the new pagan system, — the papal, — which office he assumed by virtue of his political conversion to
the political Christianity of his time, he played into the
hands of the ambitious bishops by giving them in that
Sunday law their coveted "use of the power of the State
for the furtherance of their aims" to compel men to accept the decrees, and submit to the dictates, of the
church.   He, and all others, will find that this is the
literal truth of the origin of Sunday laws.

All this is supported by abundance of testimony of
undoubted authority.   So eminent a divine as Dean
Stanley declares plainly that the retention of the old
pagan name of "*dies solis*," or Sunday, for the weekly
Christian festival, "is owing to the union of pagan and
Christian sentiment with which the first day of the
week was recommended by Constantine to his subjects,
pagan and Christian alike, as the 'venerable day of
the sun.' . . . It was his mode of harmonizing the dis-
cordant religions of the empire under one common institution."

This same mode of harmonizing paganism with
Christianity was further illustrated by his imperial
coins, bearing on one side the name of Christ, and on
the other the figure of the sun god, with the inscrip-
tion, "the unconquerable sun."   This confusion of pagan
and Christian ideas and practices is what made the

papacy, the union of church and state, and the confusion of civil and religious things, from which, with
the exception of the government of the United States,
the nations have not even yet freed themselves. This,
sir, is the authority, and the only authority, for Sunday
laws. Sunday has no basis whatever as a civil institution; it never had any. And the only basis it has, or
ever had, as a *religious* institution is in that confusion
of paganism and Christianity which made the papacy,
with all that it is or ever was.

As authority for Sunday, and as the basis of this legislation, Dr. Johnson here to-day appealed to the fourth
commandment. The " American Sabbath Union," now
in session in this city, and which is working for the
passage of this bill, likewise declares the basis of their
whole movement to be the fourth commandment. It is
proper, therefore, to inquire, What authority is there for
Sunday laws, in the fourth commandment? As this is
a question of legislation and of law, I shall examine it
from the stand-point of law. Suppose, then, that this
bill has become a law, and the courts in construing it
take judicial cognizance of the fourth commandment as
the basis of the law.

Courts are guided by certain well-established rules
in the construction of laws. According to these rules,
what would be the result of the judicial construction of
such a law upon the basis of the fourth commandment?

1. " What a court is to do, is to declare the law as
written."

The fourth commandment as written is as follows :—

" Remember the Sabbath day to keep it holy. Six
days shalt thou labor, and do all thy work: but the
seventh day is the Sabbath of the Lord thy God : in it
thou shalt not do any work, thou, nor thy son, nor thy
daughter, nor thy man-servant, nor thy maid-servant,
nor thy cattle, nor thy stranger that is within thy gates;

for in six days the Lord made heaven and earth, the
sea, and all that in them is, and rested the seventh day :
wherefore the Lord blessed the Sabbath day and hallowed it."

That commandment as written says, " The seventh
day is the Sabbath." Consequently, at the very first
step the first day of the week, as declared in the bill,
and as these people demand, would be completely shut
out.   But if any should innocently inquire, The seventh
day of what ? the commandment itself is ready with an
explicit answer.   It is the day upon which the Lord
rested from the work of creation.   In that work he
employed six days, and the seventh day he rested,
and that alone, as Dr. Johnson has said, established
the weekly division of time.   As those seven days
formed the first week of time, the seventh of those
seven was the seventh day of the week, and that is the
seventh day fixed in the commandment.   This is confirmed by the Scriptures throughout.   The New Testament itself declares that the Sabbath is past before
the first day of the week comes.   Mark 16 : 1, 2, says : —

"And when the Sabbath was past, Mary Magda-
lene, and Mary the mother of James, and Salome, had
brought sweet spices, that they might come and anoint
him.   And very early in the morning, the first day of
the week, they came unto the sepulcher at the rising of
the sun."

Those people mentioned in this Scripture came to
the sepulcher very early in the morning of the first day
of the week ; yet the Sabbath was past.   This national
Sunday-bill which is here under discussion proposes to
secure the religious observance of the Sabbath on the
first day of the week.   But such a thing can never be
done, because according to the scripture, the Sabbath
is past before the first day of the week comes.   It matters not how early persons may come to the first day
of the week and its observance, they will be too late

to find the Sabbath in it; because by the word of the Lord it is past before the first day of the week comes.

This is made yet more positive, if need be, by the record in Luke 23:56 and 24:1, which says:—

"And they returned, and prepared spices and ointments; and rested the Sabbath day according to the commandment. Now upon the first day of the week, very early in the morning, they came unto the sepulcher, bringing the spices which they had prepared, and certain others with them."

Here it is declared that certain people rested the Sabbath day *according to the commandment,* and then on the first day of the week did what they would not do on the Sabbath day. This proves conclusively that the Sabbath day according to the commandment which these men cite, and which it is supposed that the courts will have to interpret when this becomes a law,—this proves that that Sabbath day is the day before the first day of the week, and therefore plainly demonstrates that the seventh day named in the commandment is nothing else than the seventh day of the week. Therefore, if courts, in the interpretation of this commandment as the basis of a Sunday law, declare the law as written and as defined by the plain word of the Lord, they will have to declare that the seventh day of the week, and not the first day, is the Sabbath.

2. "In the case of all law, it is the intent of the lawgiver that is to be enforced."

What, then, was the intent of the Lawgiver when the fourth commandment was given? Did the Lawgiver declare or show in any way his intention?—He did. When the Lord gave that law at Sinai he did not leave it to the people to interpret it to suit themselves, nor to interpret it at all. By three special acts every week, kept up continuously for nearly forty years, he showed his intent in the law. The people were fed by manna in their forty years' wanderings. But on the seventh day of the week no manna ever fell. On the sixth day of the week there was a double portion, and that which was gathered on that day would keep over the seventh, which it could not be made to do at any other period, or over any other day in the week.

By this means the Lawgiver signified his intent upon the subject of observing the day mentioned in that law ; and keeping it up continuously for so long a time made it utterly impossible that his intent should be mistaken.

Therefore, if the courts of the United States shall ever take judicial cognizance of the fourth commandment, which is held forth by these people as the basis and the authority for their movement, according to this rule, the seventh day of the week, and not the first day, will have to be declared the Sabbath.

3. "When words are plain in a written law, there is an end to all construction : they must be followed."

Are the words of the fourth commandment plain words ? — They are. There is not an obscure nor an ambiguous word in the commandment.

Then, according to this rule, if ever that question becomes one of judicial cognizance in the courts of the United States, the seventh day of the week, and not the first day, will have to be declared to be the Sabbath. That is all that the courts can declare.

Therefore, the conclusion of the whole matter thus far is that if our courts are to remain courts of law and are to be guided by the established rules for the construction of law, they never can uphold any law for the enforcement of the Sabbath or the Lord's day on the first day of the week.

Just here, however, another element comes into court, and that is the theological. The theologians step in right here and declare that the intention of the fourth commandment has been changed, and that now, instead of that commandment's requiring the observance of the seventh day in remembrance of creation, it requires the observance of the first day of the week in remembrance of the resurrection of Christ. To reach this point they first declare that the phrase "the seventh day" in the commandment is indefinite ; that it does not enjoin the observance of any particular day, but only of one day in seven. But such a construction is not only clearly in violation of established rules for the construction of law, but it involves an assumption of power on their part that can never be allowed. Admitting for argument's sake that that phrase in the commandment is indefinite, it must be admitted that the Lord, when he wrote it, intentionally made it indefinite, because the Scripture says that when he had spoken these words, he added no more ; he had nothing more to say on the subject. What he said then was final. If, then, that statement be indefinite, he intended it so, and no other than the Lord ever can, or ever has the right to, make it definite. But the theologians, just as soon as they make it indefinite to escape the obligation which it enjoins to observe the seventh day, then make it definite in order to sustain the supposed obligation to keep the first day of the week. Consequently, when they make it definite after having declared that the Lord made it indefinite, they assume the power and the prerogative to do what the Lord intentionally declined to do ; and in that they put themselves above God.

So much for their theological assumptions. Such a course is not only theologically an assumption of almighty power, but on the basis of law it is a violation of the rule which declares that —

4. "No forced or unnatural construction is to be put upon the language of a statute."

To make the phrase "the seventh day" in that commandment indefinite, and mean any one day in seven and not any seventh day in particular, is nothing else

12

than to put a forced and unnatural construction upon the language, not only of the commandment itself throughout, but on all the language of the Scriptures upon the subject of the commandment.

Further, to make that commandment support the observance of the first day of the week in commemoration of the resurrection, is not only to put a forced and most unnatural construction upon it, but is a direct violation of that other rule of law which declares that —

5. " A constitution [or statute] is not to be made to mean one thing at one time and another at some subsequent time when the circumstances may have so changed as perhaps to make a different rule in the case seem desirable. . . . The meaning of the constitution [or statute] is fixed when it is adopted, and it is not different at any subsequent time when a court has occasion to pass upon it."

As I have clearly proved, the meaning of the fourth commandment when it was given was that the seventh day of the week should be observed, and for the reason that God rested that day from the work of creation, and blessed the day and hallowed it.   That Sabbath day for that reason was established before man had sinned, and before there was any need of the resurrection of Christ. If man had never sinned, the day would have been observed, for the reason given, in commemoration of the rest of the Creator from his work of creation.   That being the meaning of the commandment when the commandment was given, that must be the meaning of the commandment so long as the commandment remains.   And according to this rule it can never be made to mean anything else ; although to the theologians who wish to have it so, the circumstances concerning the resurrection may seem to make it desirable.

Here the question very pertinently arises, Shall the Congress and the courts of the United States adopt the wishes of the theologians, and, in violation of the rules

NO AUTHORITY FOR SUNDAY LAWS.

of law, undertake to make the statute of God mean that which it was never intended to mean? In contemplation of this demand which is now made by the theologians, the words of Judge Cooley — "Constitutional Limitations," p. 67 — are worthy of consideration by Congress, as well as by the judges of the United States courts. He says : —

"A court or legislature which should allow a change of public sentiment to influence it in giving to a written constitution a construction not warranted by the intention of its founders, would be justly chargeable with reckless disregard of official oath and public duty."

The theologians have given to the fourth commandment a construction which is not in any sense warranted by the intention of the Author of the commandment. They come to the national legislature, and ask it to allow itself to be influenced by these theological sentiments in giving to that written constitution of the government of God, a construction which is not warranted by the intention of the Founder of that constitution. As Judge Cooley says, such a thing done to a human constitution, an earthly statute, would be reckless disregard of official oath and public duty. But if this is true in the case of things wholly human and earthly, what should be thought of such an action with reference to the divine constitution, and heavenly law?

Will the national legislature allow this theological sentiment to influence it to commit an act with reference to the constitution and laws of the living God, which, if committed with reference to the laws of men, would be reckless disregard of official oath and public duty? Not only do I ask, Is the national legislature ready to do this? but is it ready also by doing it to force the United States courts into the sanctioning of it in direct violation of the plainest principles of every rule for the construction of law? Is the national legislature ready to take the step which would turn all our courts of law into courts of theology? For such would be the only effect of the enactment of such a law as is here demanded by the theologians; because when the law comes to be interpreted by the courts upon the basis upon which the law is enacted, the first day of the week as the Sabbath can never be sustained by rules of law or by the principles of interpretation established in law. The only way it can ever be sustained is by principles established by the theologians and by theological distinctions, in total disregard of the rules of law; and the effect of it can be nothing else than to turn our courts of law into courts of theology.

More than this, the Scriptures plainly and logically show the seventh day to be the Lord's day. The actual expression, "the Lord's day," is used but once in the Bible, and that in Rev. 1 : 10, saying, "I was in the Spirit on the Lord's day." But that text does not say what day of the week the Lord's day is. Other texts in the Bible, however, speak on the subject in such a way as logically to show what day is meant by the expression, "the Lord's day." The Lord himself said, "The Son of man is Lord also of the Sabbath." Mark 2 : 28.

The Lord also said, "The seventh day is the Sabbath." Here are two plain Scripture statements which may form the premises of a syllogism; thus : —

Major : The Son of man is Lord of the Sabbath.

Minor : The seventh day is the Sabbath.

The only conclusion that can ever be drawn from these premises is, —

Therefore, the Son of man is Lord of the seventh day.

That conclusion is just as sound as these two statements of Scripture are, and the two statements of Scripture are as plain and positive on that subject as any two statements ever can be made. Forming another syllogism, of which the above conclusion shall be the minor, we have this : —

Major : Whatever day it is of which the Son of man is Lord, is the Lord's day.

Minor : The Son of man is Lord of the seventh day.

Therefore, the Lord's day is the seventh day.

This logic is unquestionable ; this conclusion is just as true as the Scripture itself. Therefore, as surely as courts undertake the interpretation of any statute enforcing the observance of the Lord's day, and enter upon an inquiry as to what day is the Lord's day, they will, if logical, be brought face to face with the fact as demonstrated by the word of the Lord himself, that the seventh day, and not the first day, is the Lord's day.

But it will probably be said that the courts are not to enter upon the interpretation of Scripture ; they are to interpret the law as it has been enacted, and as it is written ; and the law as enacted says that the first day of the week is the Lord's day, and that is as far as the courts can go. Suppose that be granted. Then that puts the United States Government into the place where it establishes an institution as the Lord's and enforces its observance, which not only the Lord has not established, but which is directly contrary to the plain word of the Lord upon the subject of this institution and its observance.

One or the other of these alternatives therefore the United States Government will be forced to adopt as surely as this bill or any one like it shall ever become a law. The Government will either have to become the authoritative interpreter of Scripture for all the citizens of the Government, or else it will have to put itself in the place of God, and authoritatively declare that observances established by the State and which it calls the Lord's are the Lord's indeed, although the word of the Lord declares the contrary. Is the United

States Government ready to take either of these positions? Is the Congress of the United States ready to force the Government of the United States to the alternative of taking one or the other of these positions?

The taking of either of these positions by the Government would be nothing else than for this enlightened nation, in this period of the nineteenth century, to assume the place, the power, and the prerogatives of the governments of the Middle Ages in enforcing the dogmas and the definitions of the theologians, and executing the arbitrary and despotic will of the church.

Thus, from whatever point this subject of Sunday laws may be viewed, it plainly appears that aside from the papacy there is no authority whatever for Sunday laws, nor even for Sunday keeping; and that the only effect that a national Sunday law can ever have, will be only evil, and that continually. Let Congress now and forever decidedly and utterly refuse to have anything to do with it in any way whatever; and let all the people, instead of sanctioning a movement to bring the national legislation down to the degraded level of the States on this subject, put forth every effort to bring the legislation of the States up to that place where it shall be limited as the power of Congress is limited by the declaration of the national Constitution, that it " shall make no law respecting an establishment of religion, or prohibiting the free exercise thereof."

Now, in the name of law, Constitutional and statutory, moral and civil; in the name of enlightenment and progress; in the name of reason and the revelation of Jesus Christ, I seriously ask, Why should the people of such a nation as this, living under such a constitution as is our national Constitution, be asked to return to the papal system in the Dark Ages, which was only the inevitable outcome of the wicked scheme that was conceived in sin, — "the man of sin," — and brought forth in iniquity, — "the mystery of iniquity," — in the days of Constantine? Why should such a people as this, dwelling under the best Constitution and the most enlightened influences of all ages, be asked to return to the wicked system that characterized the Middle Ages?

No, sir; the noble men who pledged their lives, their fortunes, and their sacred honor, when they established our Constitution, separated, as they supposed forever, this nation from all the wicked influences of the church-and-state systems of the colonies, of England, and of all other nations of all times. And under this Constitution, in true liberty, civil and religious, in genuine enlightenment and progress, this nation has deservedly stood as the beacon light of the world for a hundred years. Let this splendid nation ever still look forward and not backward ; let it still hold its honored place before all the nations ; and God forbid that by any such effort as is now being made in behalf of this Sunday law, this glorious nation should be brought down from her high place, and made to follow in the papal train.

Gentlemen, no further argument is needed to show that the Sunday laws of all the States, and the principles of the decisions of the Supreme Courts which sustain them, are wholly wrong, springing from the papal principle of church and state, and supported by the equally un-American principle of the omnipotence of the legislative power. They are totally subversive of American principles. Yet Sunday laws have never been, and can never be, sustained on any other principle. And this is only to say that which is the sum of all this discussion : There is no foundation in justice, in right, *or even in expediency*, for any Sunday laws, or Lord's-day laws, or Sabbath laws, UNDER ANY GOVERNMENT ON THIS EARTH.

APPENDIX A.

THE American Sabbath Union in its "Monthly Documents," has tried to make it appear that, in my argument before the Senate Committee, I admitted the right of the Government to make Sunday laws for the public good. The effort was not only made by the Association in its own documents, but the document and statements were reprinted in *Our Day*. To counteract the influence of this effort, as well as to make the point yet clearer, if possible, and expose another method which the Sunday-law workers employ to secure support for their movement, I insert the following —

OPEN LETTER

To the Rev. J. H. Knowles, Secretary of the American Sabbath Union.

DEAR SIR : In the monthly documents of the American Sunday Association, edited by yourself, you have chosen to charge me with insincerity ; and you have also done your best to make it appear that I " admit all that the friends of the Sunday-rest law generally claim — the right of the Government to make Sunday laws for the public good."

You have garbled extracts from the report of my speech before the Senate Committee on the Sunday law, and then have italicized certain words and sentences in one passage to try to make it appear that I admit the right of the Government to make Sunday laws for the public good.

You have quoted from my speech the following words in the following way : —

"Whenever any civil government attempts to enforce anything in regard to any one of the first four commandments, it invades the prerogative of God, and is to be disobeyed (I do not say resisted, but disobeyed). . . . The State, in its legislation, can never legislate properly in regard to any man's religious faith, or in relation to anything in the first four commandments of the decalogue ; *but if in the exercise of his religious convictions under the first four commandments he invades the rights of his neighbor, then the civil government says that is unlawful. Why? Because it is irreligious or because it is immoral ? — Not at all; but because it is uncivil, and for that reason only.* [Italics ours. — ED.]"

It is in the italicizing of these words that your effort is made to make me admit what I continually and consistently denied before the committee, and do deny everywhere else. You have inserted in the above quotation three periods, indicating that a portion has been left out ; and you know full well, sir, that in the portion which is there left out, is the following : —

" *Senator Blair.* — ' You oppose all the Sunday laws of the country, then ? '

" *Mr. Jones.* — ' Yes, sir.'

" *Senator Blair.* — ' You are against all Sunday laws ? '

" *Mr. Jones.* — ' Yes, sir ; we are against every Sunday law that was ever made in this world, from the first enacted by Constantine to this one now proposed.'

" *Senator Blair.* — ' State and national alike ? '

" *Mr. Jones.* — ' State and national, sir.' "

Not only were these words there, but in that portion which you have printed following the italicized words, you yourself have printed my plain denial of the right of any nine hundred and ninety-nine people out of a thousand to compel the thousandth man to rest on the day on which the majority rest, in the following form : —

" *Senator Blair.* — ' The majority has a right to rule in what pertains to the regulation of society ; and if

Cæsar regulates society, then the majority has a right in this country to say what shall be rendered to Cæsar.'

"*Mr. Jones.*—'If nine hundred and ninety-nine people out of every thousand in the United States kept the seventh day, that is, Saturday, and I deemed it my choice and right to keep Sunday, I would insist on it, and they would have no right to compel me to rest on Saturday.'

"*Senator Blair.*—'In other words, you take the ground that for the good of society, *irrespective of the religious aspect of the question*, society may not require abstinence from labor on the Sabbath, if it disturbs others?'

"*Mr. Jones.*—'No, sir.'

"*Senator Blair.*—'You are logical all the way through that there shall be no Sabbath.'"

That last expression of mine, saying "No, sir," is in accord, and was intended when spoken to be in accord, with Senator Blair's inquiring statement whether society may not require abstinence from labor on the Sabbath. My answer there means, and when it was spoken it was intended to mean, that society *may not* do so. As to its disturbing others, I had just before proved that the common occupations of men who choose to work on Sunday or any other day do not disturb and cannot disturb the rest of the majority who choose to rest that day.

Again: A little farther along you print another passage in which are the following words:—

"*Senator Blair.*—'You would abolish any Sabbath in human practice which shall be in the form of law, unless the individual here and there sees fit to observe it?'

"*Mr. Jones.*—'Certainly; that is a matter between man and his God.'"

Now, I should like for you in a monthly document, or by some other means, to show how by any fair means, or by any sincere purpose, you can, even by the use of italics, make me in that speech admit the right of the Government to make Sunday laws for the public good. You know, sir, that in that speech I distinctly stated that any human laws for the enforcement of the Sabbath, instead of being "for the good of society, are for the ruin of society."

Again: You know, for you printed it in one of your documents, that Senator Blair said to me: "You are logical all the way through that there shall be no Sabbath." You know that in another place he said again to me: "You are entirely logical, because you say there should be no Sunday legislation by State or nation either."

Now, sir, I repeat, you have charged me with insincerity. Any one making such a charge as that ought to be sincere. Will you, therefore, explain upon what principle it is that you claim to be sincere in this thing, when in the face of these positive and explicit statements to the contrary and Senator Blair's confirmation of them to that effect, you can deliberately attempt to force into my words a meaning that was never there, that was never intended to be there, and that never can by any honest means be put there?

More than this: It can hardly be thought that Senator Blair will very highly appreciate the compliment that you have paid to his logical discernment, when in the face of his repeated statement that I was logical all the way through, you force into my words a meaning that could have no other effect than to make me illogical all the way through.

I have no objection to your printing my words as they were spoken; but I do object to your forcing into them a meaning directly contrary to that which the words themselves convey, and which they were intended to convey; and I further object to your so garbling my statements as to make it possible for you to force into them a meaning that they never can honestly be made to bear.

In that speech also I said that if an idol-worshiper in this country should attempt to offer a human sacrifice, the Government should protect the life of its subject from the exercise of that man's religion; that he has the right to worship any idol that he chooses, but that he has not the right to commit murder in the worship of his idol, and the State forbids the murder without any reference at all to the question as to whether that man is religious or whether he worships or not, with no reference to the commandment which forbids idol-worship, and with no thought whatever of forbidding his idolatry. I stated also that if anybody claiming apostolic example should practice community of property, and in carrying out that practice should take your property or mine without our consent, the State would forbid the theft without any reference at all to the man's religious opinions, and with no thought of forbidding the practice of community of property. You know that it was with direct reference to these words that I used the words which you have italicized. I there distinctly denied that the State can ever of right legislate in relation to anything in the first four commandments of the decalogue. But, if any man in the exercise of his rights under the first four commandments, and in this case under the fourth commandment, should invade the right of his neighbor, as I have expressed it, by endangering his life, his liberty, or his property, or attack his character, or invade his rights in any way, the government has the right to prohibit it, because of the incivility; but with never any question as to whether the man is religious or irreligious, and with never a purpose or a thought of forbidding the free exercise of any man's right to work on any day or all days, as he chooses.

This is precisely what every State in this Union already does by statutes which punish disturbances of religious worship or religious meetings, or peaceable assemblies of any sort. But there is a vast difference between such statutes as these and the ones which you desire shall be enacted. These are strictly civil statutes, prohibiting incivility, and are far from anything like the enforcement of religions observances. The Sunday-law workers complain of the disturbance of their worship on Sunday. If they are sincere in this, why do n't they enforce the laws already on the statute books prohibiting disturbance of worship? California, for instance, prohibits disturbance of worship, under penalty of five hundred dollars' fine and six months in jail. But instead of having such legitimate laws enforced, you propose to prohibit the disturbance of your worship on Sunday by compelling everybody to keep Sunday. Upon this same principle you would have the State forbid the offering of human sacrifices by an idol-worshiper, by compelling him to keep the second commandment. In short, the principle is that you would have the State prohibit incivility by compelling everybody to be religious. And you are so enraptured with this distorted view, that you have chosen in your sincerity and by *italics* to force me to sanction the wicked principle. But it will not work. I say always, If your worship is disturbed on Sunday or at any other time, let the State punish the person or persons who create the disturbance. Let the State punish them by such strictly legitimate statutes as the States already have on this subject. But let the State never attempt to prohibit disturbance of worship by trying to compel men to worship, nor attempt to prohibit incivility by enforcing religious observances. This is just what I had in view, and is precisely what I meant, in the words which you have italicized.

All this is further shown in the argument which I
made, in that, immediately following the words which
you have italicized, I proved that Sunday work does
not disturb the rest or the worship of those who keep
Sunday. And the conclusion of that is, therefore, that
there is no basis for Sunday laws on that ground. This
I prove by the fact that the people who make this the
ground of their demand for Sunday laws, do not recognize for an instant that work on Saturday disturbs the
rest or the worship of the people who keep Saturday.
I there showed that if your work on Saturday does not
disturb my rest or my worship, my work on Sunday
cannot disturb your rest or your worship. I made this
argument not only on this principle, but from actual experience. I know, from an experience of fifteen years,
that other people's work on Saturday does not disturb
either my rest or my worship on that day. There are
Seventh-day Adventists in every State and Territory of
this nation, in Canada, nearly every country of Europe,
the Sandwich Islands, Australia, South America, China,
South Africa, and other places. They all rest every Saturday ; they all keep it as the Sabbath unto the Lord.
But no person has ever yet heard of a Seventh-day Adventist who ever complained that his rest on the Sabbath
was disturbed by other men's work. Not only is this so,
but the Seventh-day Adventists have organized churches
in the great majority of the States and Territories of this
Union. These churches are found in country places, in
villages, in towns, and in cities. They meet for worship every Saturday ; and although, as everybody
knows, Saturday is the busiest day of the week, in the
midst of such busy cities as Chicago, Denver, San Francisco, Minneapolis, and Kansas City, these churches of
Seventh-day Adventists assemble regularly for worship ;
and no person has ever yet heard of any Seventh-day
Adventists' making a complaint that their worship was

disturbed by the work, the business, or the traffic that
is carried on by other people on that day. The fact is,
our worship is *not* disturbed by these things.

Now, sir, if all the labor, the business, and the traffic
that is done on Saturday, the day which is acknowl-
edged by all to be the busiest day of the week, — if all
this, in such cities as I have named, does not disturb
our rest or our worship, will you please explain how it
is that your rest and your worship are disturbed on
Sunday, when there is not one one-thousandth part as
much labor, or business, or traffic done on that day as
is done on Saturday?

This, dear sir, is only an additional argument, but
one which rests on the living experience of thousands
of people every seventh day, conclusively showing that
your whole theory and claim for Sunday laws break
down utterly at every point.   ALONZO T. JONES.

APPENDIX B.

THE following letter from Cardinal Gibbons to Mr. D. E. Lindsey, of Baltimore, shows from the Cardinal himself, that the counting of all the Roman Catholics of the country in favor of the Sunday law on the Cardinal's indorsement, as Dr. Crafts and the Woman's Christian Temperance Union have done, was wholly unwarranted. This is exactly as I argued before the Senate Committee, and as we have argued everywhere else. We have never blamed Cardinal Gibbons for that which Dr. Crafts and the Woman's Christian Temperance Union put upon him.

"CARDINAL'S RESIDENCE,
408 NORTH CHARLES ST., Baltimore, Md.,
Feb. 27, 1889.

"MY DEAR SIR: In reply to your favor dated Feb. 25, 1889, duly received, His Eminence Cardinal Gibbons desires me to write to you, that whatsoever countenance His Eminence has given to the 'Sunday law' referred to in your favor, as he had not the authority, so he had not the intention, of binding the archbishops, the bishops, or the Catholic laity of the United States. His Eminence bids me say to you that he was moved to write a letter favoring the passage of the bill, mainly from a consideration of the rest and recreation which would result to our poor overworked fellow-citizens, and of the facility which it would then afford them of observing the Sunday in a religious and decorous way.

"It is incorrect to assume that His Eminence, in the alleged words of Senator Blair set forth in your favor, 'signed the bill, thus pledging seven million two hundred thousand Catholics as indorsing the bill.'

"I have the honor to remain, with much respect, yours faithfully,   J. P. DONAHUE,
"Chancellor.

"To D. E. Lindsey, Esq., 708 Rayner Avenue, Baltimore, Md."

[192]

an intro is needed to explain the political, religious, economic, social environment of the nation & state & influences bringing the Sunday law to the Senate — ie an active Sunday reform movement — described by EGW or referred to by — what was their agenda?

+ how does it compare c the moral majority today?

1. elect Chr/ Congressmen
2. elect Chr/ President —
3. who appoint Chr to bench — lower courts of law
4. The Courts then reverse (Sep: Chr & St) laws + opinions written by liberal courts
   in "1960"

+ some have the pattern — the progressives — liberals legislate immorality in name of Sep Chr & St & the result is the moral majority is more likely to come in + but vote you + overturn unwise laws why unbalance Chr/St affirm

We'd love to send you a free catalog of titles we publish or even hear your thoughts, reactions, criticism, about things you did or didn't like about this or any other book we publish.

in Christian should support wise law + she be engaged in civil debate — active supports wise laws single of country & should

Just write or call us at:

TEACH Services, Inc.

not remain silent to support magazines in attacks morals or principle in society when

800/367-1998

hey it might cause a backlash by Rely majority/ moral majority

www.tsibooks.com (mor/)

ie mixture better schools

problem as Chr/ compromise more & more o be truly & her more more like it & to that extent less like the Lord Jesus; the Chr loses its moral influence fungd as salt + light in state or populace around it. Then a moral majority/ can become a minority quickly — as society grows worse new concepts Chr to preserve in society gd principles + morals.

similarly, failure to
honor & respect tradit. family of
mother + father + children & m & f

by redefining the family to include
2 same sex partners or parents
will & have this blessing of welfare of society
but can expect negt consequences
family is basis of physical & moral
development of individual

∴ anything w/ attacks the family's welfare
is deliterious to the state —
robs it of taxes — ie immorality on TV
gamblers — bread winner salary
entire goes to games of chance, therefore
raise etc + others have burden to feed them,
clothe their children etc + the USGS can be
sleep + sudden of gaming losses,
congruence for gaming to be more
regulated, lower legal age for gaming
is supposedly to & tax base for govts
but it's creating w/ end up costly & state
even more lots of resources.

To get state & society back on track
need to fight gambling + ROH abuse
smoking as unhealthy + also govts
promote family — ch's need to be
active teaching others — money —
buy state + have enough resources to
meet emergency soon to come as a
result of the immoral direction
of society is heading — Let's get active!
now start!

Honor y m & f → that y days may be long
on the earth = 1st com č promise =
⑤   (longevity - health)
∴ honoring both parents
honors the family, marr/institution by the
children & society, results in prosperity
health, - promotes general welfare of society
                which is in interest of state

⑥ ₸ Kill → need deterrent laws - capital punishment
                                    or
⑦ ₸ commit adultery → homosexuals
                        fornication
                        social purpose
⑧ ₸ Steal → { unmaintainable
              illegal using rate in   "we also get women"
⑨ ₸ bear false witness   ie (FBI, Police dept plants
libel (newspaper) - false evidence   even when no proof, we
      reporter *)   - abuse of power   manufacture it or
⑩ ₸ covet   at least try to (+)
  neighbors   is people & request   result
  gh   police   lives is in jeopardy
  house   enforces freedom
  man or

  ↳ services in chu draws poor people up +)
  pen neighborly country
  we are in a crisis model   keep & correct problems
    ordeal o them in pasts
  = very serious - even who follow the NCCS+
  economic degration - are impoverished
  Look at Mexico

but hard work → leads to to increase
    & liberty
NCCS & wishes to control ev/area of life
- can't allow free speech or freedom of the press -
is a need for a real newspaper & thoughtful
articles, well written to the moderate
viewpoint

∴ I conclude Am. is falling apart morally.
+ it will take more than a Sunday law
to correct our national moral decline.
The Sunday law itself is immoral b/c it
restricts free exercise?   (+ wrong
                                    medicine)
    relig. in scene +
violates constitutional protection - off religion
    H/ the state expression as occurred in
Europe -- (The real reforms we need?)
          social economic war,
Gambling - # steal? game of chance, $ earned by hard work. is
Smoking (# kill) squandered # game of chance + you are
    + risk CA, ea. death predicted to gain b/ chance + # covet
abortion - 3rd trimester, - as method of
   late   birth control.
          doctors need moral judgment to refuse
          if baby to along - dev'g
(# murder, honor parent)

Crime # steal, # kill # covet
         # commit adultery, rape, incest etc.
homosexuality = "disease f society, probabl whatever it
    solu - education
    (5) honor parents (m + fi)
    (6) # kill -
    (7) # commit adultery
    (8) # bear false witness - all/ motors
    (9) X # steal - stand f/ other purity + conscien
    (10)   robbers?   + moral values in society
          # covet what is j. neighbor is body
          + soul, to be used unnaturally
regi to prevent someone else ∴ is ok to have
laws eg/ homosexuality, be in military
buy society? churches, state -
"(Sh # allow civil unions ∴ is a Rt)
    w/ them they feel raising f children

Post my 95 Thesis f what is
morally wrong in America —
+ we need + require real reform
or else society will go down tubes.

— Get active! —

— excesses by govt officials
(Bill Clinton) — raise taxes on smoke — + alcohol
(Al Gore)   to help offset cost

Ch's and Temperance societies why need + she
revived today